Searching for Rainbows
A Legacy of Hope from a Grieving Mother and Her Family

Nancy Gearhart

PUBLISHED BY

Our Written Lives, LLC
San Antonio, Texas

www.Ourwrittenlives.com

Copyright 2023 Nancy Gearhart

ISBN: 978-1-942923-72-5 (paperback)
ISBN: 978-1-942923-73-2 (ebook)
Library of Congress Control Number: 2024902176

Cover Art by Reverend William M. "Scotty" Brock, used with permission.
Fonts and primary rainbow graphic licensed for commercial use.
Coloring pages and art throughout the book from Freepix.com.

Scriptures taken from the Holy Bible, New International Version®, NIV®. Copyright © 1973, 1978, 1984, 2011 by Biblica, Inc.™ Used by permission of Zondervan. All rights reserved worldwide. www.zondervan.com The "NIV" and "New International Version" are trademarks registered in the United States Patent and Trademark Office by Biblica, Inc.™

Searching for Rainbows
A Legacy of Hope from a Grieving Mother and Her Family

4

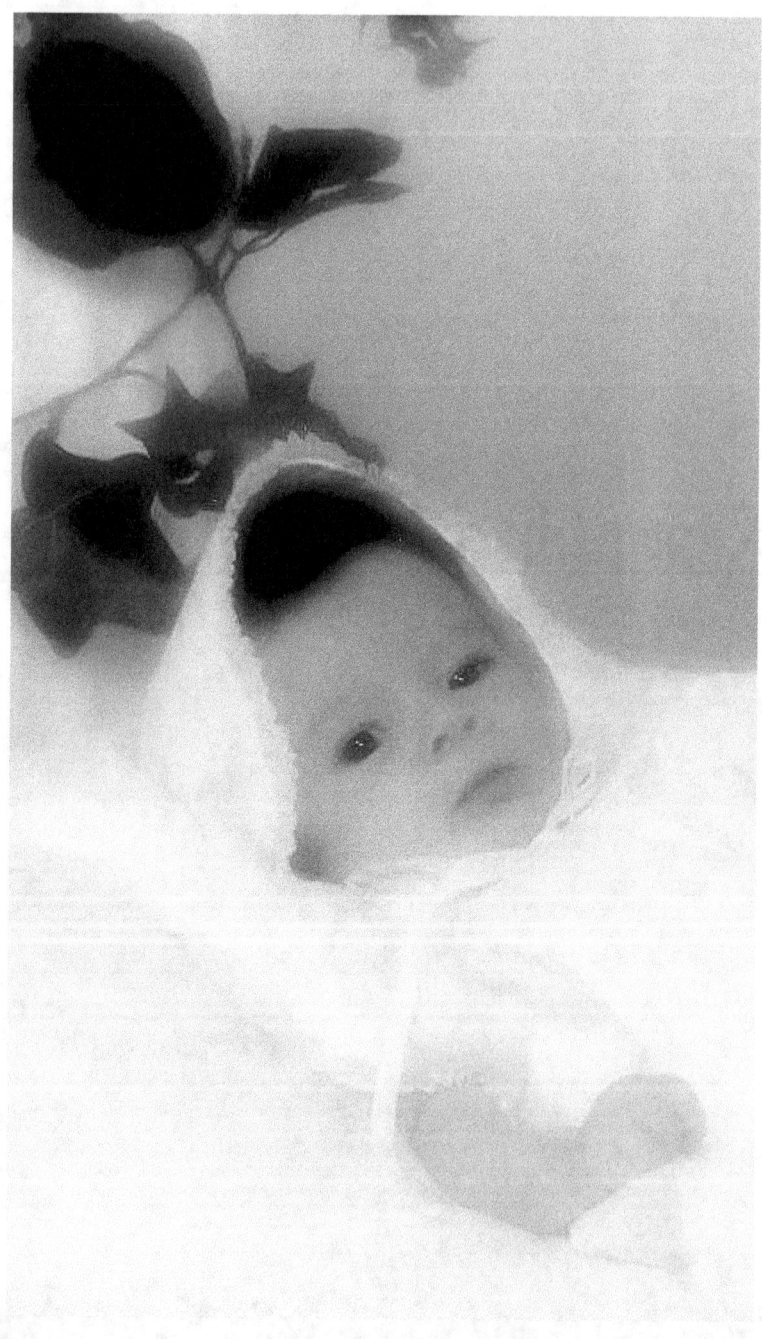

In Loving Memory of

Ansley Lynn

My sweet baby girl, your Daddy and I had dreamed of having a little girl for as long as I can remember. When you were born our little family felt complete. You were absolutely perfect.

Four months was not enough time with you, but your short life changed ours for the better, and it was your death that gave us life. I pray when you look down from Heaven and see my life, you are proud of me.

I miss you every single day. I am doing my best to honor your life by pointing others toward the only source of true peace. I cannot wait to hold you again. Till we meet again.

Love,

Mommy

A Note from the Author on
Healing Hearts

As I shared our story, I have poured out my rawest and most difficult emotions and experiences. I realize some of what I share may be difficult for you to read. I tried to stagger the chapters, alternating between the tough topics and "rainbow stories" that gave me hope along the way.

At the end of the most difficult chapters, I've included a section called "Healing Hearts" where you can interact through answering questions, or completing an exercise. I hope these mini challenges will offer some therapeutic value on your journey of healing your heart.

I do need to say, I am not a licensed counselor, for grief or otherwise, or a mental health professional. I cannot diagnose mental health conditions or recommend a course of treatment. I believe in and encourage you to seek grief counseling from a licensed counselor. If you are experiencing thoughts of self-harm, seek professional help immediately.

Contents

Acknowledgments — 11
Foreword — 14
Poem: Our Little Angel — 17
Our Story — 19
Daddy's Girl — 29

1. Why? — 33
2. Ansley's Rainbows — 37
3. Who Am I? — 43
4. Kyle's Purple Flowers — 49
5. Is It Okay to be Angry with God? — 53
6. Rainbows of Hope — 57
7. Am I Being Punished? — 61
8. Driving Through Rainbows — 67
9. Should It Have Been Me? — 73
10. Rainbows in Africa — 79
11. Do You Feel Like Running Away? — 85
12. Restoration in the Rainbows — 89
13. Feeling Alone — 93

14. Unexpected Rainbows _____ 97
15. Guilt _____ 103
16. Finding Joy in the Rainbows _____ 109
17. Regret _____ 115
18. From Storms to Rainbows _____ 119
19. Permission to Hurt _____ 125
20. Rainbows for Grandmothers _____ 133
21. It is Okay to Feel Joy _____ 139
22. Sapphire Rainbows _____ 143
23. Trust _____ 151
24. Rainbows from Canada _____ 157
25. Perspective _____ 167
26. Rainbow Families _____ 173
27. Triggers _____ 185
28. Rainbows that Bloom from Friendship _____ 193
29. Marriage in the Rainbows _____ 197
30. Rainbow Baby _____ 203

Support Ansley's Rainbows of Hope _____ 209
About the Author _____ 212

Acknowledgments

This book has taken me nearly ten years to write. I could not have done it without the encouragement of my friends and family. The pain writing brought up would cause me to put the idea of writing away for months, even years. Still, I knew I needed to finish it. I heard a sermon recently where the pastor encouraged people who weren't sure what to do next to, "Do what you know to do." Finishing this book is what I know to do.

I want to thank my husband for his love and support. Loving me was not easy after Ansley passed, but, somehow, we persevered. We beat the odds and now we have the opportunity to bless other families. Thank you for encouraging me to write and share our experiences with others who are hurting.

To my boys, you are my heart. I love you with everything in me, and I am so proud of the men you have become. By the grace of God, you are both strong, independent, caring, beautiful souls and are walking testimonies of His grace. I pray you will always seek the Lord and live for Him. I also want to thank you for bringing two beautiful young ladies into our lives.

To Hannah and Kelsie. Years before Andrew and Austin met you, I prayed my boys would find young women with a heart for the Lord. Women who would love and support them at all times. I prayed they would come from strong families and that we would have a close relationship. You both are part of a promise the Lord made to me many years ago, a promise of restoration. I cannot imagine what it was like for you to come into a family who has suffered such a traumatic loss. I know things have not always been as you may have imagined or wished, but you have made our family stronger and better. Thank you for your love, encouragement, and willingness to be a part of our journey to healing. You make our family "unit" complete.

I am so grateful for my parents. They stepped in time after time to help with the boys, despite the fact they were also grieving. They took them on vacations, let them come stay with them, and loved on them. I do not know what we would have done without their love and support.

I'm thankful for my sister, Jackie. During the time when I was first growing in my faith, she taught me how to sign the words to worship songs. That meant so much to me because I love to worship, but I am not a great singer. Being able to sign the songs gave me a special way to connect to God. Jackie also provided a place of refuge for my family when we went to visit her in Florida. It was like a little escape from the stress of our reality when we went to see her. I am so thankful for her and our relationship.

To my Tammy's Circle neighbors that became family, thank you. You were Jesus with skin on to us. Many of you sat with me on my bathroom floor or in the front yard as I screamed and cried.

You took me grocery shopping and bought us groceries. You were what the church is meant to be, and I cannot thank you enough.

I do not know where we would be today without the love and support of our church families. The priest and pastors, along with so many others, at St. Michael's and All Angels and Southside Assembly of God, helped guide us through our grief journey and point us toward our only source of hope and peace. Thank you, Father Scotty Brock, Pastor Jack Moon and Denise, and Diane and Joey Saturday. We love you so very much.

So many of our friends, church family, and loved ones blessed us during the most difficult times, but it was Melissa who drove to my home at midnight to climb into my bed and hold me when I wanted to end it all. She would come pick me up just to get me out of the house. She would let me bring her one-year-old home with me so my arms would not ache quite so bad. She let me feel what I needed to feel at the moment, and did not judge me. She is my best friend, my sister, and I could not write this book without telling her "thank you."

I wish I could name everyone who loved on us after we lost Ansley. So many drove countless hours or flew to be with us at her funeral. My husband's family drove all the way from South Dakota. No one went unnoticed, and I would not have had the courage to write our story without you. Thank you, from the bottom of my heart.

Nancy

Foreword

The prophet of old, Isaiah, wrote that God's grace can give a crown of beauty instead of ashes, the oil of joy instead of mourning, and a garment of praise instead of a spirit of despair. This book is an example of God's grace at work.

It has been my privilege to, in some small way, be a part of bringing God's grace into the lives of Nancy Gearhart, her husband Robert, and their two sons Andrew and Austin. One of the things God's grace did in Nancy's life was to turn overwhelming grief into purpose. As the Bible says, she has learned to comfort with the comfort she has received. This book is part of her purpose. She wrote it to help bring hope and comfort to those who have experienced the grief she has known all too well.

It is a story of how grace rescued the Gearhart family from the heartbreaking loss of their daughter and sister Ansley. The loss of a child, especially an infant, creates a grief that can swallow all of our hope for life. This book tells the story of what God did to help the Gearharts and what they are now doing to touch the lives of families who are in desperate need of hope.

The journey from grief to purpose has not been easy for Nancy. To find healing and hope, she had to let go of pain and despair—a difficult transaction, but worth the cost. This book is an encouragement to take the journey from grief to purpose.

As I have walked with Nancy and her family, it has been my privilege to be their friend and their pastor. Now, I also have the privilege to partner with them in sharing God's grace with families they reach with acts of kindness through Ansley's Rainbows of Hope. This book is another act of kindness.

I pray you are open to God's grace, the same grace that has changed the lives of Nancy and her family.

Pastor Jack Moon
SOUTHSIDE ASSEMBLY OF GOD
SAVANNAH, GEORGIA

Our Little Angel

Some called her a princess.
Some others a doll.
She was Mommy's little angel,
And her Daddy's all.

She always wore pink,
No other would do.
Which outfit today?
Perhaps she'll wear two.

Her hair was jet black,
So cute with a bow.
Her eyes always sparkled.
How we loved her so.

She lit up the room
With each little smile.
She was never unnoticed,
Not by a mile.

Our angel had grown tired,
And wanted to sleep.
We begged her to stay.
How we wanted her to keep.

Oh, how we wish
We could see her once more.
Her smile and her laugh,
How long to Heaven's door?

Take care of her, Lord,
With all of Your might.
Love her and kiss her,
Our angel, so bright.

*In loving member of my
precious angel, Ansley.
Love, Mommy*

Our Story

Our lives would never be the same after Father's Day 2001, the day our Ansley Lynn was born. This is our story.

My husband, Robert, and I desperately wanted a baby girl. We had two amazing boys, but we felt like something, or someone, was missing. In 2001, I found out we were having a girl, and we were overjoyed!

As excited as I was, I could not help but be a little anxious about her heart's development because our youngest son was born with a congenital heart defect. His cardiologist told us any other children we may have only had a four percent chance of being born with a heart defect, but I was still concerned.

I had several Level II Ultrasounds, specifically looking at the baby's heart. Every ultrasound read as normal, a fact I later looked at as a blessing.

I had a scheduled induction on June 17, 2001, Father's Day. Ansley's godmother was my best friend, Melissa; she was also my nurse the evening before I had Ansley. I could not sleep because of the anticipation, and once contractions began it was impossible to rest. It was wonderful having Melissa with me during that time.

My mom and sister were in the corner of the room when it was time for me to push. Melissa was on one side of me, and Robert was on the other.

Ansley was perfect. She was 7 pounds, 19 inches long, and had a head full of the most beautiful dark hair I had ever seen. The joy that filled the room was palpable. Her daddy followed as nurses took her to the warmer and then to the scale.

As Melissa and the on-duty nurse checked her out, I asked, "Is she okay? How does her heart sound?"

They both said, "She is perfect."

That was all I needed to hear.

While I was giving birth, Ansley's other set of godparents were watching our boys who were six and eight years old. They all came to the hospital shortly after Ansley was born. Her brothers were enamored with her! Austin had won a tiny gray stuffed animal that afternoon and was so excited to give it to his new baby sister. It felt as though my heart was actually smiling at the sight of my boys loving on their baby sister.

The day after her birth started out perfectly. My mom and grandmother brought the boys up to be with us at the hospital. They were wearing their *Big Brother* shirts and Ansley had on her *Little Sister* shirt. Robert ended up taking the boys out for a while later that day to give me time to rest.

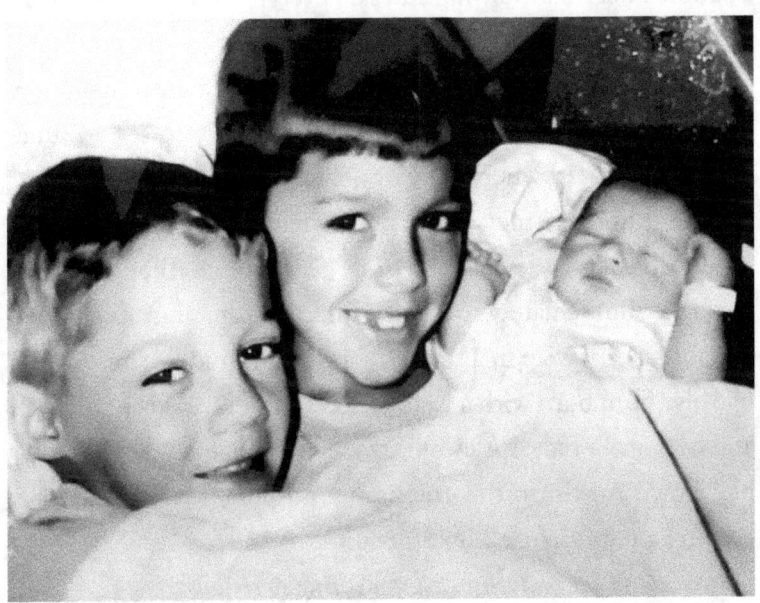

At that time, the hospital offered photography for families with new little ones. As my mom and I sat on the side of my bed looking through a brochure of picture packages, a nurse walked in to take Ansley for her hearing test. I thought nothing of it; I knew she would only be gone for a minute. Mom and I continued browsing the options, laughing at the cheesy newborn pictures.

After about 15 minutes, there was a knock on the door. It was one of the neonatologists at the hospital I worked at. When I saw who it was, I knew something was terribly wrong. She did not go to see a parent unless there was something wrong.

"Ansley turned blue during her hearing test," she said as she knelt next to the bed.

My thoughts began to race, though no words formed in my mouth. *There is no way I am hearing this.* The pediatrician had examined her that morning and said everything was good. *Surely, there has been a mistake.*

But there had not been a mistake. The next time I saw my beautiful baby girl, she was hooked up to monitors, had tubes hanging out everywhere, and was on a ventilator.

The cardiologist met with us in a small conference room and explained that Ansley had a serious heart defect. They would fly her by jet immediately to the Children's Hospital in Augusta.

Robert and I were in a state of shock. Our middle son, Austin, had also been born with a heart defect, but we had been told over and over again that Ansley's heart was normal. Six years ago, they had flown Austin to the exact same hospital. We were literally reliving a nightmare all over again.

How could they have missed something so serious?

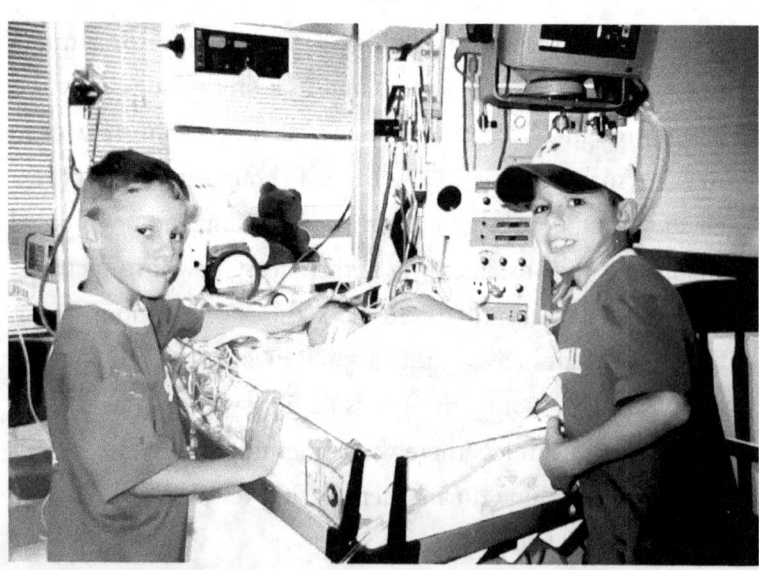

Two hours felt like an eternity as we drove to the hospital. We barely spoke a word. Once we arrived, we ran straight to the pediatric intensive care unit (PICU). The nurse who met us in the lobby was one of the nurses who had taken care of Austin. She remembered us.

They were still taking care of Ansley and setting things up, so we had to wait. My hands were shaking. They were asking me questions, but I could not think straight.

What had we done to have to go through this again? I did not think I would survive.

The PICU physician met with us and confirmed our worst nightmare; Ansley had a serious heart defect called *Hypoplastic Left Heart Syndrome (HLHS)*. Her heart defect was one of the only types that could not be repaired. The surgery she would have would "rewire" the plumbing of her heart, but not fix it. It would combine two of her great blood vessels into one. It was dangerous, and one of three major surgeries she would have. It was all so overwhelming and confusing.

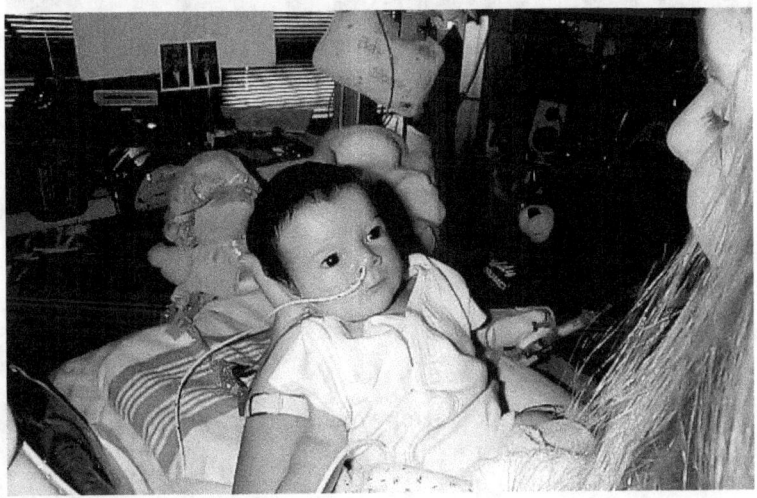

Ansley had open heart surgery when she was only five days old. The surgery went well, but she suffered many complications during the weeks afterward. She spent all summer in the hospital, but she was finally able to come home in August.

Overall, Ansley was doing better than expected. She was gaining about a half a pound per week, and the cardiologist was optimistic about the possibility of a different second surgery than what was planned, which would give her a better quality of life.

Ansley was a happy baby. She loved her daddy and her brothers, and they adored her. She had them all wrapped around her little finger. Whenever they walked into the room, she would get the biggest grin on her face.

She loved when her daddy bathed her and washed her hair. She loved going on walks, being outside, and watching her brothers run around. Life was *almost* perfect.

I wish I could share more happy memories with you, but most of what I remember took place on October 24, 2001. After numerous trips to the pediatrician's office, for what I was told was just a cold, we ended up in an ambulance with Ansley in respiratory distress. She had turned blue after I gave her a breathing treatment at home. Once we made it to the hospital, they told me she was stable and sent her upstairs to the pediatric intensive care unit.

The next time I saw my baby girl, doctors and nurses were all around her performing CPR. All of the monitors hooked up to her were flashing, and all I could do was beg her not to leave me.

I held on to her little foot and just begged. I begged the doctors not to stop trying to save her and begged God for a miracle. But they did stop, and the miracle did not come. After being home only two short months, Ansley went to be with Jesus.

I immediately fell to the floor screaming, begging God to give me a miracle. I did not want to live without her. I held her in my arms for hours praying for the Lord to take me home with her. I just wanted to die.

The next few weeks and months were more than I could bear. My arms literally ached; they should have been cradling my baby girl, but instead, they were empty.

I prayed God would take me, to stop the unrelenting pain and guilt. I replayed the events leading up to that night repeatedly in my mind. I was literally driving myself crazy. I blamed my husband for not being with me when she went into respiratory distress, the doctors at the hospital for not doing their jobs, the pediatrician for not insisting she be admitted to the hospital in Augusta, and God for not saving her.

Most of all, I blamed myself. I blamed myself for pulling her feeding tube, for not insisting the doctor admit her to the hospital, and for not calling 911. I am a nurse; I should have known better.

Grief consumed me. I felt like my world just stopped. I felt like I could not breathe. I felt I was suffocating. I thought many nights about taking the entire bottle of sleeping pills. I needed help.

I questioned things I had believed in my whole life. Like, is heaven a real place? Or is it just something we made up to help us cope with life and death?

I begged my priest for proof of Heaven. After reading through some Bible scriptures, he handed me a story written by a mother who had lost her young son to a brain tumor. That story gave me hope. That story, along with my own, is the essence of this book.

If you have experienced a loss like mine, I know this book will not take away your pain. Only time, faith, and prayer can help heal your broken heart. My prayer is that you gain confidence in heaven to help you along your grief journey.

As I share my journey to healing, may you find peace, comfort, and everlasting hope that comes through faith in God our Father. Believe His word, for it is truth.

These are just a few scriptures that remind me I will see my Ansley again.

> But Jesus said, "Let the little children come to me and do not hinder them, for to such belongs the kingdom of heaven." Matthew 19:14

"In my Father's house are many rooms; if it were not so, I would have told you. I am going there to prepare a place for you. And if I go and prepare a place for you, I will come back and take you to be with me that you also may be where I am. You know the way to the place where I am going." John 14:2-4

And he said to him, "Truly, I say to you, today you will be with me in Paradise." Luke 23:43

Daddy's Girl

My name is Robert, and I am Nancy's husband. If you are reading this book, you are likely looking for answers just as I was.

I had so many questions. *Why did I lose my child? How could a good God allow this to happen? Why her and not me?*

I begged Him to bring our baby girl back. I begged Him over and over to take me in her place.

I wish I had the answers to these questions, but I do not. The truth is, I know I will not get my answers this side of Heaven. It took years for me to accept this fact, but I trust God is good and I trust in God's plan.

Let me tell you about my Ansley. She was my missing piece. We have two boys God blessed us with; however, we longed for a baby girl. When we found out Nancy was pregnant, we were excited and nervous at the same time.

Austin, our youngest son, was born with a congenital heart defect. Even though we were told there was only a four percent chance any future children may have a heart problem, we were concerned. When we found out we were having a girl, I could not have been more excited. Nancy had several tests during her pregnancy, and we were assured Ansley's heart was normal. We were over the moon!

Ansley was born on Father's Day 2001. What a perfect day for her to be born! She was the absolute best Father's Day gift I would ever receive. She was beautiful with a head full of hair and big dark eyes. She was the perfect mix of Nancy and me. We were in awe.

Twenty-four hours later, everything changed. I had taken the boys away from the hospital for a while when I got the call. Ansley had turned blue during her hearing test, and I needed to get back to the hospital immediately.

I was in shock. *They told us her heart was perfect. How could this be happening?* I drove as fast as I could to get back to the hospital. My heart was beating so fast, and my head was spinning with questions. I had to be with my wife. I had to be with my baby girl.

When I arrived, Nancy was in a small conference room outside the Neonatal Intensive Care Unit waiting for the doctor to come. From previous, experience, I learned it is never a good thing when they have you in a private room like that one. I braced myself for tragic news.

As we sat on the small couch with our hands clasped together, the pediatric cardiologist walked in. He sat across from us saying our baby girl's heart was not right. He believed she had Hypoplastic Left Heart Syndrome but would be flown to the Children's Hospital in Augusta to be sure. If this is what she has, she would require immediate open-heart surgery. I was devastated. I asked God, "Why?" There was only silence in response.

Ansley spent all summer in the hospital, but we were finally able to bring her home. As excited as we were, having her home was hard on both of us, especially on Nancy. She had to take care of Ansley so much while I was working. In addition to caring for our boys and doing all the things she did for the house, she was giving Ansley medications through a central line in her chest multiple times a day.

Ansley had a CADD pump to administer medications. Nancy also gave Ansley medications through the tube in her nose, as well as feeding her through the feeding pump. She was overwhelmed. I would come home from work and see Nancy exhausted and hurting because she was depleted.

After being in a hospital with Ansley all summer, and then coming home to this, Nancy never had time to recover. To complicate things, she was also dealing with her grandmother being in hospice.

On the weekends when I wasn't at work, I would take care of Ansley as best I could. Nancy would go see her grandmother at the hospice and try to rest. I would take Ansley out to go shopping or to a park with the boys. I remember her looking at me with those big brown eyes and could imagine her saying, "That's my Daddy."

Our family loved the movie The Wizard of Oz and had just watched it. I would playfully ask Ansley, "Are you a good witch or a bad witch?" Ansley would get a big, goofy grin on her face, and it would melt my heart. She had me wrapped around her little finger, and I am convinced she already knew it. I so wish I had more memories like this one I could share.

Losing Ansley was one of the hardest things we have faced. For our family, we chose to press through our grief with the Lord. I cannot imagine trying to do so without Him.

I pray this book helps fill you with hope and eases the struggle of faith in your mind. I want you to know that what you are feeling is completely normal and okay. It may not feel like it at this moment, but you will make it.

Be blessed and know we are praying for you.

Love, Ansley's Daddy,

Robert

CHAPTER ONE

Why?

Why? It is such a simple question, but, oh, how I wish there was a simple answer! I know I must have asked "why" a million times.

Why did she die?

Why didn't God answer my prayers?

Why didn't God give me the miracle I longed for?

Why had He forsaken me?

There had to be a reason, right? There has to be some sort of logic behind why any child would die, right?

Why would a child be born with a congenital defect? Why would a child be diagnosed with cancer? Why would a driver decide to drive under the influence, and cause an accident that takes a child?

There has to be some sort of answer that can bring peace to hurting parents, isn't there?

For me, I had to learn to trust God and His plan. I had to believe He knew what was best, and that He was good. It took *years* for me to learn to trust God. There are still days when I question, but

I know from the very depths of my soul I would not spiritually be where I am today had I not gone through losing my child. I would not be writing a book offering you hope. I would not have started our nonprofit, Ansley's Rainbows of Hope. I would not have had the opportunity to meet the families Ansley's Rainbows serves or to pray with them.

Losing Ansley changed my life. Yes, it even wrecked my life for many years. But now I know, with every fiber of my being, I will see my baby girl again. She is waiting on her mommy, cheering me on, cheering for her dad, and for her brothers.

When you think about life in the midst of eternity, life is just a blink, a whisper in the wind. Eternity is forever. We will be with our loved ones *forever*. Your child is in heaven right now and is cheering you on as you search for hope and peace until you are reunited.

Take comfort in knowing you have not walked this dark road alone. The Lord has been beside you, weeping with you, and holding you close. The Word tells us in Psalms 56:8 that the Lord keeps track of all our sorrows. He has collected all—not some—of our tears in a bottle, and He has recorded each one in His book. Our suffering has not gone unnoticed. He has not abandoned us. It may feel He isn't there at times, but He has always been there.

When I started Ansley's Rainbows of Hope, the Lord gave me the scripture 2 Corinthians 1:3-4.

. . . Lord Jesus Christ, the Father of Compassion and the God of all comfort, who comforts us in all our troubles, so that we can comfort those in any trouble with the comfort we ourselves receive from God.

What greater way to honor your child than to be a blessing to someone else? I challenge you to step out this week and be the light someone else needs. I promise if you shift your focus off your grief and focus your attention on being a blessing to someone, you will start to feel a change within your spirit. Perhaps you thought the light within you was forever snuffed out, but when you reach out to others, it will start to kindle the flame again.

Let today be a new beginning for you.

Lord,

I lift up the mothers and fathers reading this prayer right now. You know each of them by name. You formed them in their mothers' wombs. You knew each of them before they were even born. You chose them to walk this road for a specific purpose.

I pray You will give them the strength and courage to step out this week and be a blessing to someone in need. Put someone in their path, even if it is just someone needing encouragement.

I pray, Lord, that You will let them know they are not alone. Let them know You have them in the palm of Your hand.

I ask all this in Your precious Son's Name, Jesus.

Amen.

Healing Hearts

Who do you know that needs a kind word or a hug today? Maybe you know of a need you can meet. Has the Lord brought someone to your mind?

If you are not ready to pick up the phone or visit in person, try writing them a card, or sending a text or email. I loved getting letters in the mail, especially in the beginning of all I went through.

Use the space below to write a list of people who need prayer or a blessing.

_____
_____
_____
_____
_____
_____
_____
_____
_____
_____
_____

CHAPTER TWO

Ansley's Rainbows

No parent should have to bury a child, period. If you are reading this book, I understand it is likely because your child has passed, or because you know someone who has a child who has passed. Let me start by saying, you are not alone.

I realize you may feel as if you are alone, but if you are a believer in Jesus Christ, He is with you. He will carry you through what will likely be the worst storm of your life. In Isaiah 43:1-5, God tells us:

> . . . Do not fear, for I have redeemed you; I have summoned you by name; you are mine. When you pass through the waters, I will be with you; and when you pass through the rivers, they will not sweep over you. When you walk through the

fire, you will not be burned; the flames will not set you ablaze. For I am the Lord your God, the Holy One of Israel, your Savior; I give Egypt for your ransom, Cush and Seba in your stead. Since you are precious and honored in my sight, and because I love you, I will give people in exchange for you, nations in exchange for your life. Do not be afraid, for I am with you . . .

Let that sink in for a minute. In fact, take a moment and read that scripture again. Do you see it? We will suffer in this life, but it will not destroy us; Jesus is with us. He knows you by name, and He loves you. So, take heart, you are not alone, and remember that after every storm, regardless of how devastating, there comes a rainbow, a promise of God's faithfulness.

As you may have read in the preface, after my Ansley passed, I was in desperate need of proof that Heaven was a real place and that my baby was there. I cannot adequately describe the searing, crippling pain I was feeling as a mother. My arms literally ached from not having my baby to hold.

I needed someone, anyone, to throw me a life preserver. I was drowning in my own tears. I needed help. I needed hope. I wanted to know my Ansley was waiting on me and that, for certain, I would see her again.

Yes, I grew up in church. Yes, I had been taught "Jesus loves the little children," but during my grief, I began questioning the very things I had believed in my whole life. Proof from God was the only thing I could think of that would give me the strength to face this life without Ansley.

It was about a month or so after she had passed when I received my first rainbow from God. I pray as you read about these glimmers from Heaven, which I call Rainbows, that your heart is filled with hope and with an assurance that Heaven is indeed a real place, and God is still on the throne.

One afternoon, not long after losing Ansley, I had to take the boys to the pediatrician. It was just a routine check-up, but I was dreading it. I was terrified of seeing or hearing a baby. The sound of a baby crying triggered me to suffer a panic attack. I was having panic attacks on a regular basis—in the grocery store, and everywhere I encountered a baby. If you have never experienced a panic attack, let me tell you, they are crippling.

The pediatrician's office staff had us wait in the trauma room for our appointment because there were so many patients in the office that day. My senses were on high alert, and the medicinal smell of the room reminded me of being in the hospital with Ansley. Just as we were about to leave, I heard a baby cry.

My heart began racing. I was having trouble breathing. I could not focus. It felt as if the room was closing in on me. I honestly felt as if I was either dying or losing my mind. I had to get out of there. My eight-year-old, Andrew, had to handle checking us out as I dragged Austin, who was six at the time, out to the car. I cried most of the way home.

The boys were in the backseat and did not understand what was going on. All they knew was that their mom was sad all the time, and anything could make her cry. Andrew quickly learned that mentioning Ansley brought me to tears, so he held everything in. Austin drew pictures of Ansley daily and hung them all over the house.

As we were approaching our exit on the way home, a song started playing on the radio that we used to play for Ansley when she was in the intensive care unit at the Children's Hospital in Augusta, Georgia. It was a song from her Baby Bach CD. We used to play it to help calm her heart rate and help her rest. Isn't that exactly what I needed at that moment—a calm heart and rest? The fact that this song was playing on the radio at that very moment was a miracle from God.

Just then, Austin looked up at the sky and said, "Look, Mommy, there's Ansley!" He was pointing to a perfect, tiny rainbow in the blue sky. There were no clouds that day; it was completely clear, yet there was a tiny rainbow.

I knew it had to be a sign from God. Why else would there be a rainbow in the sky on a perfectly sunny day? So here we were, driving home, listening to the song we played for Ansley in ICU, and staring at a rainbow.

I was in awe. God cared enough for me to catch Austin's attention and to remind me that my baby girl was okay. She was with Him. That rainbow did not take all of my pain away, but it did give me hope—hope that I would see my baby girl again.

The Bible tells us repeatedly that we will face storms in this life, but it also tells us in Deuteronomy 31:6, "... *the Lord your God goes with you; He will never leave you nor forsake you.*"

Psalm 30:5 promises us that our "... *weeping may last through the night, but joy comes with the morning.*"

Emotionally, I was not yet ready for joy. I felt a tremendous amount of guilt. I wish I could tell you I had unshakable faith, but at the time, I did not. I was a Sunday Christian, at best. Regardless, I had hope, and I held onto that rainbow with everything within me.

CHAPTER THREE

Who Am I?

I think the question I dreaded the most in the beginning was, "How many children do you have?"

What was I supposed to say?

Initially, I said, "I have two boys with me and a daughter waiting on me in Heaven."

As you can imagine, I faced a million questions I did not want to answer. I quickly shortened my response to, "I have two boys at home." I felt so bitter.

How could people look at me and not know a part of me was missing?

I also hated when people asked how I was doing. What did they expect me to say? "Oh, I am great? How are you?"

One time, when someone asked me how I was doing, I responded, "Well, I did not run my car into the bridge when I went under it, so I guess pretty well."

I would hear about someone else losing a child, and I would ask how old they were. If the child was older than Ansley, I would think, "At least they had more time than I did." If their child was younger than Ansley was when she left me, I felt as if their pain could not possibly compare to mine.

I had lost my compassion. I had lost who I used to be.

I became a nurse because I loved to help people. I hated the thoughts I was having, and the anger I felt toward others. I should have felt empathy for them, but I didn't. I hurt to my core. I did not know how to find "me" again, but God knew.

Five months after Ansley had passed, my neighbor asked my husband, Robert, and I to attend a Tres Dias weekend. Tres Dias is a three-day spiritual retreat designed to strengthen one's relationship with the Lord. My neighbor had spoken about the retreat often, but I was not sure it was the place for me. She was Pentecostal, and to be honest, she scared me to death. At the same time, I was drawn to her. She had a joy I did not understand and an unshakable faith. It was because of the strength I saw in her life that we agreed to go.

After the first day, I wanted to leave. People were sharing their testimonies, and all I could think about was how my story was so much worse. That afternoon, however, I mentioned something about my grandmother having been at hospice while we were having our table discussions about a testimony we had just heard.

The lady who was sitting across from me at the table asked me when my grandmother was at the hospice. Then I remembered. My grandmother had died only days before my Ansley.

I jumped out of my seat and ran out of the room. I just wanted out of there. It all felt so overwhelming.

My friend and neighbor who had sponsored me to attend the retreat, along with one of the pastors ministering that weekend, found me sitting on the steps outside and asked me what was going on.

I explained I had met the lady sitting across from me at the table before. I did not realize I knew her until she asked me when my grandmother was at the hospice. She was the same lady who was visiting her loved one in the room across the hall from my grandmother at the hospice. She had met my Ansley!

I would sit out in the hall sometimes when my grandmother was sleeping, and that same lady would come and sit with me.

Up until that time, I had felt God was punishing me, and that He didn't care about me. Yet here this woman was. I knew two people on the entire campground of the retreat, and here was a woman who had met my Ansley.

Maybe God does care . . .

I had never had a "God moment" before, and I was spooked. I did not understand what was happening. Somehow, my world was aligning with God's comfort.

The Lord set me up that weekend. He showed me He loves me, and He was not punishing me by taking Ansley. I was learning I could not find myself until I found God.

Surviving the loss of my child was not something I could do with my own strength. I had to learn to lean on the Lord. I began going to Bible studies, became more active in our church, and volunteered at every Tres Dias I was asked to serve. I drew closer to God, and slowly found my compassion again. It took years, though. I am not trying to make light of my healing process at all. I can honestly say I just stopped feeling like a victim in 2014, thirteen years after Ansley's death.

In the beginning, I lived minute by minute, then hour by hour, then day by day, month by month. My grief days turned into episodes and began to drift further and further apart. I may always have triggers that make me sad, but they aren't as crippling as they were in the beginning.

For many years, I felt guilty for any joy I felt. That was the enemy of my soul trying to steal my joy. I had to learn not to feel guilty about having a good day.

At some point, you will be able to remember your child, smile, and focus on the good times. Don't let the devil steal those moments because he certainly wants to.

The Word tells us in John 10:10, *"the thief comes only to steal and kill and destroy,"* BUT it also tells us *"Jesus . . . came that [we] may have life and have it abundantly."*

I found comfort in the scripture 1 Peter 5:10. *"And after you have suffered a little while, the God of all grace, who has called you to his eternal glory in Christ, will himself restore, confirm, strengthen, and establish you."*

He will give you strength. He will restore your home. Lean on Him.

Dear Lord,

Thank You that You never leave us or forsake us. Thank You that You walk with us through the storms of this life.

Lord, we need you. We cannot survive the pain of losing a child without You. Please carry us through this time, and give us signs, wonders, and dreams that confirm our child is safe with you.

I pray that each person reading this will receive their very own "rainbow" from You. I pray peace will wash over them and a well of hope will spring forth within them.

Thank you, Lord, for loving us.

Amen

Healing Hearts

My challenge for you this week is to write down your favorite memory, or memories, with your child. Think of something that will make you smile and hold onto that, even if it is just for a moment. Allow yourself that time to feel joy.

_____
_____
_____
_____
_____
_____
_____
_____
_____
_____
_____
_____

CHAPTER FOUR

Kyle's Purple Flowers

The week after Ansley passed, I was desperately searching for answers. I went to our church and met with Father Brock in the sanctuary. With tear-filled eyes, I begged him to be honest with me.

"Is Heaven a real place? Or is it just something we have made up so we can cope with death? Promise me Heaven is a real place!"

He said, "Nancy, Heaven is real. I will be right back." He rose from the pew and went to his office. He emerged just moments later with a paper in hand. It was a story from the niece of one of the parishioners. Her story about losing her son, Kyle, changed my life.

The woman's name was Lana Hill, and she called me shortly after I read her story. We talked and it helped me so much. I've shared her story with many people I've worked with through

Ansley's Rainbows of Hope, and I want to honor her for allowing her story to help so many people.

Nine years later as I started writing this book, I tried to find her, to no avail. She had remarried and moved away. I'd like to share her story, the one she had printed and shared with so many people through our church. I've rewritten it here to save space. I've changed the perspective to the third person so I could tell it using my voice, but I used direct quotes from the original printed version I have from her, as well as bits of dialogue from our phone conversation.

Kyle was born in August of 1989. He was Lana's third son and reminded me a lot of my Austin in the way she described him. He was always into something and had energy for days. In May of 1996, Kyle's first-grade teacher asked her class to write in a journal. I'm sharing what he wrote, including his original spelling.

He wrote, "I wuld go in a storm, and I wuld be brave, I will be week, to be ded."

The teacher showed the story to his mom, and Lana asked Kyle what it meant.

Kyle responded, "I will go into a storm, and I will be brave. Then I will be weak, then I will be dead."

A few weeks later, Kyle was sleeping next to his mom when he started to moan and cry.

"He was having a bad dream and protested loudly, 'I want to go home!'" Lana told me she gently woke him up, and told him, "You *are* home, baby."

"No, I want to go home to Heaven!" he said to her.

One month later, Kyle was diagnosed with an inoperable brain tumor. At six years old, he faced a terminal diagnosis. Lana never had to tell Kyle he was dying; he told her.

"When will Jesus come to take me home?" he once asked her.

She told him, "When you see Jesus, grab His hand and don't look back."

I could barely read the next part of the story as I was sobbing, but it was the part that blessed me beyond measure. Lana described how Kyle saw angels in his room keeping vigil. He named them John and Anna. One day, Lana asked Kyle if the angels could see her as well. He was looking up at them, so Lana waved towards the ceiling.

Kyle broke into a huge smile and said, "They're waving back!"

"Kyle had many dreams and visions of Jesus," Lana shared. "He told me there are flowers in Heaven with colors he has never seen before. He said that Jesus was as big as a building and each time Kyle saw Him, Jesus knelt down, handed Kyle an apple, and hugged him."

One morning Kyle woke up very excitedly and said, "Mom, I saw an angel with your face, and she is so beautiful!"

Kyle passed away a short while later. The last word he spoke was "Jesus."

Before Kyle passed, Lana asked him how she would know he was okay. He told her to look for "a new purple flower" and that would be her sign that he was well.

Many new purple flowers have grown around their home since that time. Even to this day, when Lana sees a purple flower, it reminds her to be strong. As a tribute to Kyle, she tries to live by a modified version of his words:

*I will go into a storm, and I will be brave.
Then I will grow strong, and then I will survive.*

When I spoke with Lana shortly after I read her testimony, she confirmed every word of the story I read was true. She was the first mother I spoke with who had lost a child, and she understood where I was and what I was experiencing. She was such a blessing to me. For the first time, I had hope and a bit of comfort knowing that Heaven truly is a real place and that my Ansley is there waiting for me.

CHAPTER FIVE

Is it Okay to be Angry With God?

Losing Ansley shook my entire world. After the shock wore off, it was easier to feel anger than the pain of loss.

I was angry at the EMTs that drove us to the hospital, the ER doctors, her cardiologist, her pediatrician, Robert for not being with me when she went into respiratory distress, myself for failing my daughter, and the list goes on and on.

I felt mostly betrayed by God. Why had He not saved her? I know He could have, but He chose not to. I was angry with God.

Things just did not make sense to me. If He is a good God, a good Father, then how could He let a child suffer? How could He sit back and watch a child die? Why was she born with a congenital heart defect?

I had these questions in my mind and heart but would not voice them; I was scared to. I already felt as if God was mad at me. I felt His taking Ansley was punishment for something. I thought if I said how I really felt, He would take my boys too. I did not realize He already knew my thoughts before I ever spoke the words. He knows our hearts.

You may be feeling a similar way that I felt. You may be asking God why some children get the healing their parents pray for, while others do not. Why are some delivered from substance abuse and others are not? There are so many hard questions. You may be feeling angry at God for not giving you answers.

The thing is, God can handle our anger. He will not love us any less if we express anger toward Him. The Word does not tell us to not feel anger. It tells us not to *sin* in our anger.

Check out some of the Psalms, such as Psalm 109, and the book of Job. People cried out in anger, and in Job's case, God still called him righteous. You cannot really be angry with someone you do not know, so anger is a part of relationship.

God desires a relationship with you. Seek Him. Ask Him the tough questions. No, you may not get the answer you are looking for, but when you truly seek Him, you will find Him.

I also want you to take comfort in knowing that anger is a very normal part of the grieving process. We feel angry because someone we love has died. We have question, after question, after question that goes unanswered and fuels our anger.

You want your child with you, period. Honestly, there is no answer that will satisfy your shattered heart. So, for now, I'm giving you permission to feel the anger. Scream, yell, punch a pillow, cry it out, whatever you need to do. I used to beat my rocking chair cushion as hard as I could. If you feel you need to throw or break something, go outside and go for it.

I remember taking a bat to the nebulizer in my driveway. You have no idea the relief that came from beating that thing until it was in pieces. Remember, I was giving Ansley a breathing treatment with that nebulizer when she went into respiratory distress. I am sure the neighbors thought I had lost it, but I did not care. It was what I needed to do.

Do whatever you need to in each moment. Well, do anything that does not involve you hurting yourself or someone else, or breaking the law. God still loves you even though you are angry with Him. Just as you love your children when they are angry with you, God won't stop loving you. Eventually, you will be able to channel your anger into something good. Just look at the mother who started MADD—Mothers Against Drunk Driving.

My challenge for you this week is to start a journal. Writing can be very therapeutic and can help you get in touch with your true feelings. I tend to write like I am writing a letter to God, or sometimes a prayer to God. You can write however you feel comfortable, but I promise it will help. You will be amazed at how far you have come when you go back and read your journals. The journey to healing can be beautiful if you let God in.

Father,

Thank You for loving us even when we are angry with You. Thank You for Your mercy and grace. You see our broken hearts and all You desire is for us to seek refuge in You. Help us to do that. Help us to run to You, to curl up in Your lap, and cry while You love on us. You are our Anchor of Hope, Lord, and we love You.

Amen

Healing Hearts

As you color the picture, meditate on this promise from God's Word. "We have this hope as an anchor for the soul, firm and secure . . . JESUS . . ." Hebrews 6:19-20

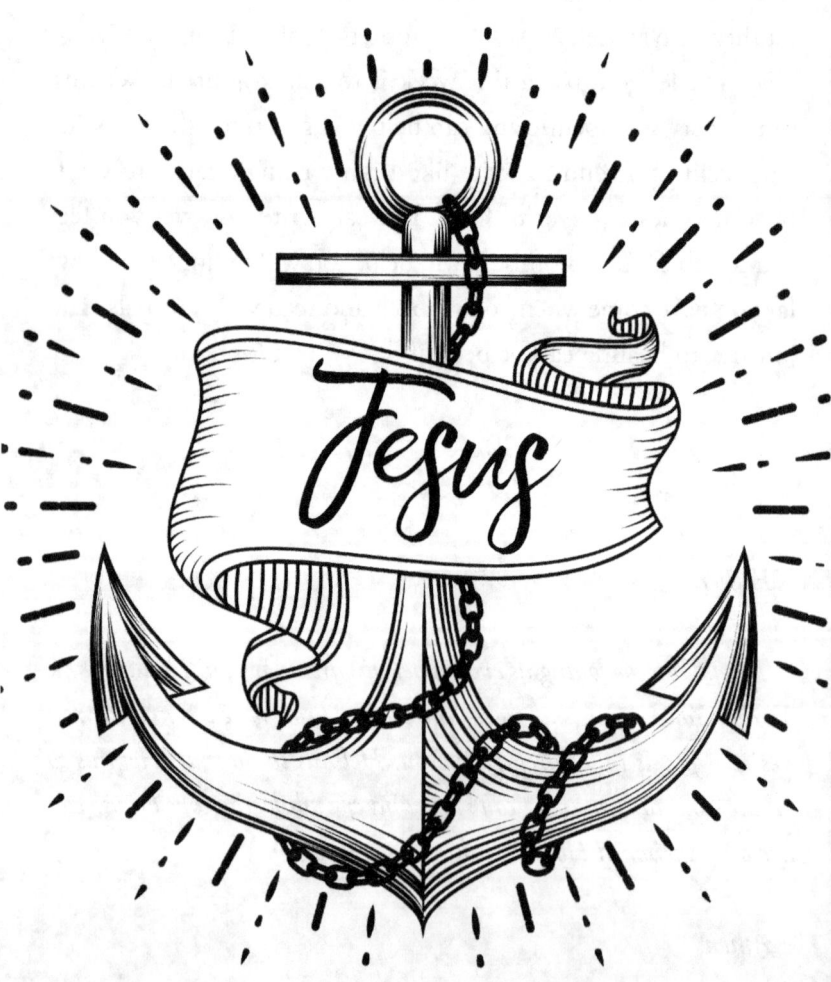

CHAPTER SIX

Rainbows of Hope

Not long after the incident at the pediatrician's office, the boys were outside playing with their neighborhood friends. It was a beautiful fall day. There was a gentle breeze blowing with leaves bustling about. I could hear the kids laughing and playing. To anyone else, it was a perfect day. To me, it was just another day I had to survive.

Our home was often the central hub for the boys and their friends to hang out, and that day was no different. The little girl from down the street came knocking on my door a short while later. She was only four or five years old. It was not uncommon for kids to show up at our house and knock—they were often tattling on one another, but this time it was different.

I slowly made my way to the door. I really did not want to see anyone. As soon as I opened it, the little girl started to talk very fast.

"Ansley and Austin's older brother, Andrew, is in the drain by the road!"

"What do you mean Andrew is in the drain?" I felt all the blood rush out of me, and panic started to set in.

The little girl grabbed my hand and pulled me out to the street. My heart was beating so fast, I thought it was going to burst. How could this be happening again?

The drain was only 50 feet or so from my door, but it felt like an eternity had passed until we reached it. The girl pointed to the drain by the road and insisted Andrew was in there.

I fell to the ground screaming for Andrew, but he wasn't answering me. I just knew he had drowned. I frantically tried to lift the lid that covered the drain—to no avail.

It wasn't long before my next-door neighbor came running outside.

"Miss Nancy, Andrew is not in the drain! He's back there!" She pointed to the drainage ditch. I looked up and saw him. He and his friends had been yelling at the little girl through the canal pipe and she honestly thought he was in the drain.

I ran into the house screaming. Even though Andrew was fine, I was terrified of losing another child. I went straight to my bathroom and fell to the floor, rocking back and forth, curled up in a ball.

Andrew came running in there and just held me. My sweet Andrew was only eight years old. Robert ran into the bathroom, not understanding what had happened. I could not speak. The fear of losing another child was paralyzing. Andrew held me as he was crying, saying over and over again how sorry he was and that he was okay. All I could do was cry and rock.

Austin came into the bathroom not long after Andrew, insisting we come outside. We followed him out into the front yard. He stopped, pointed up toward the sky, and there they were . . . not one, but two tiny rainbows!

It was another perfectly clear day. There shouldn't have been rainbows in the sky. It was a miracle. Those two tiny rainbows filled me with hope. They reminded me that God had not forgotten me. They were a promise from the Lord that He would protect my boys. I was able to breathe again.

Thank You, Lord, for my rainbows of hope.

CHAPTER SEVEN

Am I Being Punished?

I did something today I was not sure I would ever be able to do. I read the journal I wrote after my Ansley passed. I cried all the way through it. Reading that journal stirred up my emotions as if I was experiencing losing her for the first time. It is crazy how raw my heart still feels after so much time has passed.

One of the saddest statements I read in my journal was, "It is like a terrible nightmare. My beautiful baby is now hooked up to all kinds of machines: IVs, a vent, etc. Why is God punishing me?" I remember believing with everything in me I was being punished for something.

I remember one of the nurses asked me, "What did you do to deserve this?" She had taken care of our son, Austin, and then later Ansley. The way she spoke to me validated my belief that God was punishing me. I thought to myself, *"Even this nurse thinks I deserve what is happening to me."* I can hear her asking me that question to this day.

Sometimes, in the midst of the worst times in our lives, people will become tools of the devil to add to our pain and validate the lies that bombard us without them even realizing it. It is especially difficult to combat these types of thoughts when you are already struggling and afraid. I do not think the nurse is a malicious person, but I do think people need to think before they speak. What she said hurt me.

Back then, I was a Sunday Christian at best, and my view of God was warped. I saw Him as a mean judge, ready to smite anyone who did anything contrary to the Bible. In my eyes, He was not a loving God.

My daddy died from cancer when I was only two years old, and the little sister, whom I so desperately wanted, was born deaf. I believed God was out to get me, and I thought I deserved all the hardships of my life. I remember when I was little, I asked my mom why God hated us and she responded, "I don't know." Her answer showed me that she too believed He hated us for all that happened.

It was not until 2014 that I realized I had been separating God and Jesus in my mind. God was cruel; Jesus was love. I know it sounds crazy. I understood Jesus was God in human form, but somewhere along the way, I viewed Jesus as compassionate, and God as a judge. It was not until I started sincerely seeking a relationship with God that my view of Him started to change. How can you have a relationship with someone you do not know? I had to get to know God through reading His Word.

Certain scriptures really spoke to me. Genesis 50:20 states, "You intended to harm me, God intended it for good." God intended it for good. It was like a light bulb went off. Satan tried to take my family out, and I almost let him, but God had another plan.

Romans 8:28 promises that ". . . in all things, God works for the good of those who love Him, who have been called according to His purpose."

In Joel 2:25, He promises us, "[He] will repay you for the years the locusts have eaten . . ."

I started to view the tragedies of my life differently. As Jeremiah 29:11 tells me, God had a good plan for my life, but Satan had a plan as well. If Satan was not scared of the plan God had for us, He would not bother with us. All I could think was that God must have something amazing in store for my family, and that gave me hope. I still hold onto that same hope today. I know God will restore what is broken and change our brokenness into something beautiful if I have faith. His Word does not lie.

I learned God was not punishing me, and I want to tell you He is not punishing you. He uses trials to prepare us for His plan for our lives. We have to trust His plan and not our pain. That is hard to do.

You also have to know that you have a real enemy out there, Satan. The Bible tells us in John 10:10, "The thief comes only to steal, kill, and destroy," but here is the good part, "I have come that they may have life, and have it to full."

I pray you can grab hold of this anchor of hope sooner than I did. I nearly drowned in the storm of my grief, but I am so thankful He saved me. He will save you too.

If you are struggling to trust God, I urge you to start searching the Bible and really get to know God the Father. I also suggest you seek out a Christian grief counselor. My grief counselor was God-sent. I am not sure where I would be without her. There is no shame in getting professional help and I highly recommend it.

Father,

Your Word tells us over and over again how much You love us. Right now, it doesn't feel that way. Help me see beyond my pain to Your promises. Let me know You are near. Send friends, family, and even strangers to be Your hands and feet. Help me to see Your love in the actions of others. Guide me as I search scripture and allow Your Holy Spirit to minister to my wounded soul.

Thank You, Lord, for who You are.

Amen

Healing Hearts

As you reflect on what you have just read, search the Bible for God's promises that speak to your heart. Use the space below to write out scriptures or verse references.

God's promises . . .

1.
2.
3.
4.

Romans 8:28

Today, God is saying . . .

Lord, help me to remember . . .

1.
2.
3.

CHAPTER EIGHT

Driving Through Rainbows

In 2010, we learned our youngest son, Austin, who was fifteen at the time, needed a pulmonary valve replacement. That meant open heart surgery again.

The congenital heart defect Austin was born with was called Tetralogy of Fallot. His defect was much different from Ansley's in that it could be repaired.

Austin suffered many complications following his first surgery as an infant, including cardiac arrest. He underwent 45 minutes of CPR with me in the room screaming and pleading with them not to stop. His being alive today and on no cardiac medications is a miracle in and of itself.

Still, I was terrified. I did my best to hide my fear from Austin because he was also scared. He was a teenager and aware of what he would be going through. He knew his sister died from complications related to her heart condition. Having his fear on top of mine was almost more than I could bear.

The surgery would be in the summer of 2011, so when our oldest son, Andrew, graduated from high school that spring, we decided to celebrate in St. Lucia. We went zip-lining through a rainforest, rode horses on the beach, snorkeled in the ocean, and had a great time. It was just the distraction we all needed from thinking about Austin's upcoming surgery.

As scared as I was, I knew God had Austin in the palm of His hand, and I knew He had a plan for him. By all accounts, Austin should have died after his first surgery as a baby. The fact that he was alive was a miracle. I held on to the scripture found in Jeremiah 29:11, *"For I know the plans I have for you, declares the Lord, plans to prosper you and not to harm you, plans to give you hope and a future."*

Even as I held onto that promise, God knew my heart was struggling. I confided in my best friend, Melissa. She had walked with me through losing Ansley, and she was there for me during this scary time with Austin as well.

Melissa worked at a surgical center in Atlanta and knew the Physician's Assistant for the pediatric thoracic surgeon who would be operating on Austin. That connection was a sign to me that God saw right where we were.

The PA called me at home one evening and answered all my questions. She was amazing. She helped calm my nerves and ease my anxiety. She even visited us at the hospital after Austin's surgery.

Austin's surgery went extremely well. Friends and family surrounded us the whole time. People drove hundreds of miles just to sit with us and pray.

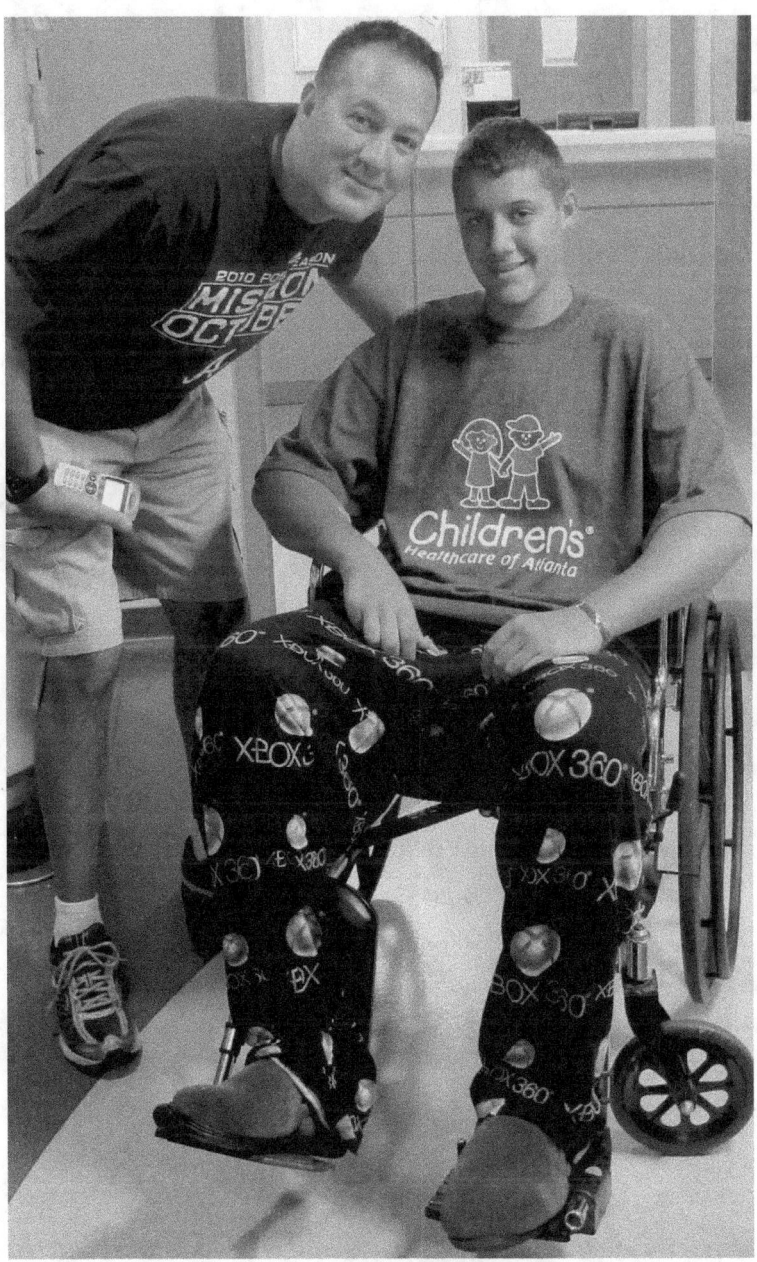
Robert with Austin at the hospital.

After only four days in the hospital for open heart surgery, we were on our way home! Praise God! But it was what happened on the way home that left us speechless.

It was a beautiful day outside. As we were driving down the interstate, we saw a HUGE rainbow that formed a bridge over the road. To the left of the rainbow was a cloud that looked like the form of an angel, but it was not just any angel. It looked just like an angel we had all seen before.

Shortly after Ansley passed away, the priest from our church, Father Scotty Brock, painted a picture of an angel. The train of the angel's robe painted a trail of a rainbow across the sky. He called the painting "Ansley" and gave it to us. The cloud beside the rainbow we saw on the road that day after Austin's surgery looked exactly like the angel in the painting.

We must have spotted the rainbow and the cloud angel at the same moment because Robert pulled the car over to the side of the road without saying a word.

We all got out of the car in complete silence. It was such a holy moment. We were all just in awe.

To think the Lord would do something like this for us was beyond our comprehension. God loved us. He had not left us or forsaken us. We were so thankful. God was letting us know, "I've got this! Trust in Me alone!"

The rainbows on the highway after Austin's surgery.

The cloud angel.

CHAPTER NINE

Should it Have Been Me?

by Austin Gearhart

My name is Austin Gearhart. I am the middle child of Robert and Nancy. As you just read, I was born with a congenital heart defect and underwent open heart surgery twice. I do not remember the first surgery, as I was only a year old, but I knew it was a miracle that I was alive. My mom told me the story of my heart stopping three days after my surgery and undergoing 45 minutes of CPR many times. I know it is only by God's grace and love I am here today.

I was six years old when my sister was born. I do not remember much from that time, but I do recall climbing into her crib and taking her out. I carried her into the kitchen and Mom about had a heart attack. I remember feeling so connected to my sister because we both had broken hearts and we both had scars down the center of our chests. I was devastated when she died, and I wondered if the same thing would happen to me.

My senior year of high school was a very rough time in my life. I was angry at the world and God. I wanted to join the Army like my dad, but because of my heart condition, I could not. I wanted to go to college at North Georgia, and again, because of my heart, I could not.

I had struggled to get through school, and now there was a chance I would not even be graduating high school. I wrestled with thoughts that my parents hated me and maybe it would just be better if I wasn't there. I questioned whether it should have been me who died instead of Ansley; maybe my parents would have been happier. The idea of committing suicide entered my mind. I now know all of these thoughts were lies from the enemy but at the time I was full of fear about my unknown future.

For a short season, I turned to drugs and alcohol to take the pain away. It was easier to numb the pain than to confront how I felt with my parents. The Lord protected me during that time, and I am so thankful I never became addicted to substances. I did fall away from my family, though, and even further away from God.

Later that year, a pastor from our church passed away. My mom would not allow me to be left at home alone, so I had to go to the funeral with her. During the service, they played a song by Israel & New Breed called "Your Presence is Heaven." They intermixed the song with powerful sermon clips by the pastor who had passed. I broke down crying and felt compelled to walk to the altar. I cried out to God to save me. He did!

As I began to search the Word, I came to Daniel 3:8-25 and read about three courageous men named Shadrach, Meshach, and Abednego. The familiar story brought me hope. King Nebuchadnezzar appointed them to be over the affairs of a province in Babylon. The story talks about the king making a decree for everyone to bow down and worship a false idol.

Shadrach, Meshach, and Abednego did not follow the king's orders. The three men knew that there was only one God, and even though they were about to die, they had faith that God would save them—one way or another.

They were sentenced to die in a fire that the king ordered to be stoked seven times hotter than normal. The fire was so hot it instantly killed the guards who bound the three men up and tossed them in.

When the King looked at the fire, he was amazed to see the three men were unharmed and walking around in the fire. To his amazement, he also saw a fourth man he said, "Looks like the son of God."

I know at times it may seem as though God has forgotten you and you're being thrown into a fire by yourself. That is exactly how I felt; however, just as God was with those men in their fire, He was with me, and He is with you.

I want to encourage you. Whenever you feel alone in your struggle and pain, pray God reveals Himself to you. My mom prayed that prayer and God sent rainbows as a constant reminder that her baby girl was with Him. Ansley is safe, healed, and loved. God can send you your own "rainbow," a sign that is personal between you and the Lord. It will be a reminder to you that He has never left your side.

I would also like to say something about your other children. When Ansley passed, I knew my parents were grieving, but it hurt me that they were emotionally absent. During that time, I questioned their love for me. I would like to suggest that you often remind your surviving children you are thankful they are with you and remind them how much you love them.

My parents didn't purposefully make me feel unloved while they were grieving, but I still felt that way and I needed to forgive them so I could heal. I forgave my parents a long time ago, but there was still more to let go of. Sharing my story here and telling my parents how I felt at the time has brought even more healing to our relationship.

Everything we went through as a family helped shape me into who I am today. I love Jesus. I put Him first in my life, and I want to serve Him. My mom always told me the Lord had a special call on my life, but it was not until the day I surrendered my life to Jesus that it became real to me personally and I believed He had a plan for me.

Dear Heavenly Father,

Thank You for always being with me as I walked through the fire. Thank You for always being there, even when I was not looking for You.

I pray that if the person reading this book feels any form of guilt for surviving, they will release it in Jesus' name. Help them to know they are meant to be right where they are. Reveal Yourself to them in a new way. Send them their own rainbows as a reminder they are never alone.

In Jesus' name, I pray. Amen.

Healing Hearts

Take some time to appreciate the life and beauty that is around you. Simple things, like coloring, can help you connect to shapes and colors, noticing them in your daily life.

CHAPTER TEN

Rainbows in Africa

by Austin Gearhart

Despite the fact I had given my life to Christ, I was still lost when it came to knowing what I needed to be doing in this world. I did graduate high school, but I did not do well at the first college I attended.

My mom came home from a Bible study she was attending one evening and said our pastor mentioned we should look into something called Youth with a Mission, or YWAM, for short.

As Mom and I sat side-by-side at her computer watching a video we found online about the program, we both had chills. There was no doubt that going to YWAM for Discipleship Training was my next step. There were campuses all over the world I could travel to, but I had my heart set on going to YWAM in Tennessee. The campus was beautiful, and it was the perfect distance from home. The Lord, however, has quite a sense of humor. Tennessee may have been where I wanted to go, but it was not where the Lord ordained for me to go.

As I opened the acceptance letter, I was surprised to see I was not going to Tennessee, but to Texas. As I packed for the five-month discipleship program, I had no idea what to expect. I was excited and nervous, full of anticipation.

My parents drove me to Texas, and as we pulled onto the campus, we all had an unexplainable peace. My mom was devastated she was leaving me, but I was ready. The teaching and friendships I made during my time at YWAM were life-changing, but it was the outreach I was most excited about.

There were five countries to choose from. I was wavering between going to China or Romania, but when it came time to write down my choice, I knew I was called to another place entirely.

I was so excited to tell my parents! I did what any young man does and called my mom. Well, let's just say she was not as enthusiastic about it as I expected.

"Uganda? In Africa? Wait, where is it exactly?" She pulled it up on the map and busted out crying. Uganda was surrounded by a lot of hostile areas that were in the news at the time.

"You never once mentioned Uganda! What happened to China or Romania?"

I explained when it was time for us to make our final decision, Uganda was where I was called to be. Did I mention it was my mom's birthday when I told her? My dad was not too happy with me because she spent most of the day crying. Oops.

Honestly, I did not realize the fear Mom wrestled with over something happening to me or my brother. I knew I needed to go to Uganda, despite her feelings. We would both have to trust the Lord to protect me.

The first few days in Uganda were incredible. Everything was so different from the States. We took some short tours through the village of Kampala to help us learn about the area we would be ministering to. On my last tour, I met a man and his sister. The man introduced himself as Pastor Richard.

The pastor kept staring at me. He then pointed to me and said, "You were supposed to die when you were a baby." I was in shock. *How did that man know that? He did not know me!* I had never met him or spoken to him, but somehow, he knew I almost died when I had my heart surgery!

He continued, "You were supposed to die, but God saved you, and as you continue to preach the word of God, your voice will be healed!"

I have always struggled with my voice because, after my heart surgery, I was left with a paralyzed vocal cord. My voice is raspy, and it is very noticeable. When I meet anyone new for the first time, they always ask, "Are you sick?"

I shared my story with Pastor Richard. He prayed over me and told me how God showed him how the enemy tried to take me out. He said I was never alone, and angels had surrounded me even as a baby in surgery.

It was the first time I had ever experienced such a strong God moment like this, and I was awestruck afterward. God still spoke through others. God truly was with me. God was real. Now, when people ask me if I am sick, I use it as an opportunity to share my testimony.

In one region of Uganda, we stayed in huts. One evening as I was returning from outreach, a huge rainbow stretched over the top of the huts. It was a beautiful, clear day. I took a picture and as soon as I had Wi-Fi, I sent the picture to my mom. I could not wait to tell her about the pastor and the rainbow the Lord sent me!

Uganda will always hold a special place in my heart. It is not only where I saw the Lord perform miracles, but also where I fell in love with my wife, Hannah. She was on the same mission trip I was on. We became friends when we were in Texas, but seeing the Lord work through her and the amazing heart she has for people, made me realize she was the one for me.

I left Uganda with a sense of purpose, acceptance, and a desire to serve others. I knew I wanted to go to college, and I knew I would marry Hannah someday. I am so thankful for the Lord's mercy and grace. He shows up at the most unexpected times and in the most unexpected ways. He is always here, and He is with you right now.

A rainbow over Austin's hut in Uganda.

CHAPTER ELEVEN

Do You Feel Like Running Away?

After Ansley died, I remember wanting to get in my car and just drive. I did not care where I went. I wanted to get as far away from reality as possible, and never look back. I guess I hoped I could outrun my pain. If only it were that easy.

I was lost. I was a stranger in my own home; it was no longer the safe place it had once been for me. The sadness there was tangible and suffocating. I hurt all the time and wanted to escape. I wanted to get out of there.

I may not have physically left, but my soul was crushed and often absent. I was an empty, broken shell. I would try to be a wife to my husband and mother to my children, but it was a struggle. Emotionally, I had shut down. I did not want to be alone, but I did not want to be around my family either. It was too painful. It is a miracle my marriage survived, and my boys turned out as wonderful as they did. I attribute our family solely to God's grace.

Ansley passed on October 24. Halloween was just a week away. I could have cared less about it, but my boys cared. My mom had made doctor costumes for them, and my best friend had snagged masks and booties from work. At six and eight years old, they were so excited to trick-or-treat. I reluctantly helped them get dressed, and my neighbor took them door-to-door with her children.

All I wanted to do was curl up in a ball, cry, and sleep the pain away. I will be honest, I felt angry my kids even wanted to go trick-or-treating. Why didn't my family hurt the way I did?

I should have been thankful they didn't feel the level of pain I felt, but that is not where my mind was at the time. I resented anyone who could go on with their life while grief was swallowing me alive. Yes, that meant I even resented my boys.

I am so ashamed I thought that way. Satan had me bound, and I could not see any light or hope. It was a horrible place to be. I pray you do not let him trap you the way he trapped me. The Bible promises us in James 4:7, that if we will recognize the enemy, submit ourselves—our grief, anger, resentment—to God, and resist the devil, he will have to flee!

I am so thankful I did not run away. I am a firm believer we must go through whatever we are going through, to get through it. Running away would have only postponed my grief. That is the same reason I chose not to take antidepressants. Please hear me when I say that some people need antidepressants, and they should take them if it works for them. Antidepressants made me feel nothing—I felt numb. I knew if I did not go through the pain of grief in the moment, I would have to at some point.

Was that the right decision? I will never know, but I do know I am in a much better place than I was, and I have seen the Lord turn my loss into something beautiful. Running away is never the answer. Get help. There are Christian grief counselors available. Run to a Christian counselor; run to Jesus; run to the church;

run to a trusted friend or family member, but do not run away. I promise you will regret it if you run. You will have no regrets if you stay and face your situation with the people you love.

Lord,

Sometimes my pain is too much for me to bear and I want to run away. Comfort me in those moments. Remind me I am not alone. Breathe life into me through your Word, for I know it is alive and brings healing.

Lord, the families reading this are hurting and some feel like they are dying inside. Please be with them. Send them their very own rainbows. Let them know their child is safe in your arms and waiting on them in Heaven. Love them and shower them with your peace.

We love you, Lord.

Amen.

Healing Hearts

Color the picture as you meditate on the Word of God.

"May the God of hope fill you with all joy and peace as you trust in him, so that you may overflow with hope by the power of the Holy Spirit." -ROMANS 5:18

CHAPTER TWELVE

Restoration in the Rainbows

As my relationship with the Lord grew, I wanted to see the Lord turn what the devil meant to harm me into something good. I began praying for direction. I knew there had to be a purpose in all we went through, but what was it? The Bible tells us in Romans 8:28, "And we know that in all things God works for the good of those who love him, who have been called according to his purpose." Notice it says ALL things, not just some things.

2 Corinthians 1:3-5 says that God wants us to comfort others as He has comforted us. On April 23, 2014, the Holy Spirit kept me awake all night, flooding my mind with His plan. This book was part of that plan. The second was to donate part of the money from the book to families of critically ill children.

When Austin was in the hospital for those three months in 1996, we were a young, poor, military family. I had to stay in

Augusta with Austin the entire time, and Robert would drive up to see us on weekends. There were many times we could not afford for him to make the trip. Other times when he did drive up, we could not afford to buy meals.

The Lord reminded me of our financial hardships during that horrible time. No parent should have to worry about how they are going to pay for a meal when their child is fighting for their life. I could see the ministry God was calling us to. My heart was aching to bring some kind of comfort to families going through the same sort of situations I faced with my children.

Starting a non-profit is no easy task. When I first started researching how to do it, I was quickly overwhelmed, and like any grown woman, I called my mom crying. She told me she had started non-profits when she worked at a lawyer's office and was honored to help me. She was sure the attorney she worked for would love to help as well.

My husband, Robert, and I, with the help of my mom and her priest, started Ansley's Rainbows of Hope the very next month. Again, I was amazed at how God was in the details. I truly believe my mom went to paralegal school in her 50s for the very purpose of helping us start Ansley's Rainbows of Hope.

As I prayed about the ministry, God began revealing more and more. I would quickly write down whatever I believed came from Him. The mission statement was one of the first things He gave me.

The mission of Ansley's Rainbows of Hope is to ease the financial burden experienced by families of critically ill children receiving care at a distant hospital. Meeting their financial needs was the means to fulfilling the vision He gave me. The vision was to offer Christian love and hope to the families of these critical children as we met financial needs. We want parents to be able to focus on their sick or injured child, not on how they are going to pay for a hotel or their next meal.

I knew what God wanted us to do, but how in the world would it work? How would we get referrals? Where would the referrals come from? I decided to call the pediatric intensive care unit at our local hospital and spoke with a nurse before she transferred me to the nurse manager. We talked about the ministry and decided we would have lunch to work out the details.

We talked for at least 20 minutes before I asked her how long she had worked there. I told her Ansley had passed away in 2001 at the same hospital where she worked. She told me she knew who I was. She was one of the nurses that had cared for Ansley that night!

She remembered Ansley was in the first room on the right, and she told me the nurse I had spoken with on the telephone earlier was the other nurse in the room with Ansley. She said every so often they would ask one another, "Do you remember that beautiful baby that came in with the dark hair?"

Of all the patients, they remembered my Ansley who was only in there for about an hour. It was another sign from God that His hand was all over what we were doing. I felt chills all over my body, and tears welling up in my eyes.

I asked the nurse manager if she was the nurse who came back in the room that night and sat on the floor in front of me while I rocked Ansley after she passed. She was! I told her that most of what happened after Ansley passed was a blur, but I remembered her coming back in there and sitting there trying to comfort me.

God is so good. I am amazed to this day at His faithfulness and how He brought this woman back into my life. It was one of many confirmations we received as we began this journey.

Seeking the Lord's will for your life will bring so much healing and peace. For me, to know that Ansley's story may bless a hurting parent gives me such joy. Her life, as short as it was, meant something! Since we started the organization, we have had the opportunity to help hundreds of families. Meeting their financial need is only one piece of what we do.

We try to meet with the families in person because we have walked in their shoes; we get it. We know what it is like to live in a hospital room for days and months on end. We spend time getting to know them, and we pray for them. I cannot tell you what a blessing it has been. The Lord does not allow us to walk through these storms in vain. He will use the storms of life to direct us to our ministry if we allow Him. I pray you will!

Logo for Ansley's Rainbows of Hope.

CHAPTER THIRTEEN

Feeling Alone

Some of the loneliest times of my life were the days and weeks after Ansley's funeral. I felt abandoned. Everyone had returned to work, school, and life, yet my life had come to a crashing halt. My home went from constantly filled, to completely empty. I was alone all day surrounded by the nauseating scent of flowers from the funeral home, a constant reminder of all I had lost.

The only time my phone rang was when Robert, my mom, or my best friend called to check on me. No one else knew what to say. A part of me did not want to talk anyway and was grateful I did not have to. There was another part of me that desperately wanted to talk about what happened, but I could not talk to those closest to me. I was consumed with grief. If I talked to anyone else who was grieving Ansley, I felt overwhelmed by their grief on top of mine.

Unable to talk to Robert about what I was feeling created tension in our marriage. He did not understand why I could talk to my grief counselor or even my friend's husband, but not to him. I did not understand it myself, so I could not explain it to him.

I felt alone and there was nothing anyone could have said to make me feel any better. The loneliness I felt came from losing Ansley, not from being physically alone. I needed someone I could confide in, but I felt that unless they had lost a child themselves, they could not understand the depth of my pain.

People can only relate to grief on a level they have experienced. While the loss of a spouse, friend, or parent is devastating, it is not the same as the death of a child. I remember my grief counselor telling me there is no greater pain than losing a child and I agree. Parents are not supposed to bury their children, period.

I wish I had known the scriptures more intimately at that time in my life. If I had scripture memorized in my heart, I would have known the Lord had not left me. I would have known that when I pass through the waters, He is with me; and when I pass through the rivers, they will not sweep over me. When I walk through the fire, I will not be burned; the flames will not set me ablaze. These are promises from God found in Isaiah 43:2. His Word is the same today as it was when it was written.

God was there with me the whole time. He carried me through the darkness, even when I wasn't aware He was there. I was not alone, but I did not feel God's presence because I was not seeking it. I spent my days asking "Why?" instead of asking Him to comfort me.

There is no right or wrong way to grieve, but knowing what I know now, I would rather grieve with Jesus than without Him. Without Him, there is no hope. With Him, we have the assurance that we will see our children again.

If you are struggling and feeling alone, ask the Lord to reveal Himself to you in a tangible way and expect to see Him work in your life. His love and comfort may come in the form of a friend calling to check on you, an unexpected visit, or a letter in the mail. God will send people to be the hands and feet of Jesus for you.

The comfort God sends may come in the form of a rainbow, as it did for me. God will speak to you in a way that makes sense to you. He is faithful and He will let you know you are not alone.

If you do not have someone you can reach out to, there are support groups and grief counselors available, even online and through social media. My appointment with my grief counselor was the one thing I looked forward to each week. A counselor can throw you the life preserver you so desperately need. Whatever you decide, do not walk the road of grief alone. Let Jesus comfort you and find someone you can lean on.

Lord,

Thank You for never leaving us nor forsaking us. Thank You for walking through the fire with us and making sure we are not burned.

I lift up the parents reading this right now. Comfort them like only You can, Lord. Let them know that although they may feel alone, they are not alone. You are right there with them. Let them feel Your loving arms around them.

I pray You will give them a tangible sign that You are there, just as You did for me.

In Jesus' Name, Amen.

Healing Hearts

What does it look like for you to not feel alone?

_____
_____
_____
_____
_____

DEUT. 31:8

NEVER ALONE

CHAPTER FOURTEEN

Unexpected Rainbows

After Ansley passed, I began to think of all the things I would miss out on. I would never help my daughter pick out the perfect outfit or send her off with her daddy on a father-daughter date. We wouldn't pick out a prom dress together, and I would never teach her how to apply make-up. I wouldn't get to watch her fall in love, go wedding dress shopping, or see my husband walk her down the aisle and dance with his baby girl at her wedding.

There were so many memories we would never make. In the early years after Ansley passed, Robert and I dreaded going to weddings. The father-daughter dance was a reminder of all we had lost. We could not get past our grief to celebrate the moment at hand.

In early 2014, the Lord gave me the word "Restoration" to focus on, sort of like a theme word for the year ahead. In my mind, restoration meant I would have another baby, but I was in my 40s. I did not really want to start over again with a newborn, but even after all the time had passed, I still wanted a baby girl.

Just as the first glimpse of sunlight emerges from a stormy sky, the surprise appearance of a beautiful rainbow brings joy, hope, and wonder. God began restoring my family through unexpected rainbows. In 2015, the Lord brought two young ladies into my life who would eventually become my daughter-in-loves. The girls were as different as can be, but each possessed qualities I imagined my Ansley would have. Together, Hannah and Kelsie complete our little family.

Hannah loves to bake. We swap recipes, and we are both obsessed with all things sourdough. She loves the Lord and is gentle, witty, and compassionate. She has a generous and giving heart, and her inner beauty matches the beauty she has on the outside. Hannah is also a nurse, and I love it when she calls to tell me the crazy things that happened at the hospital that day.

Kelsie could barely boil water when I first met her. She is goofy, loyal, and feels deeply passionate. She is one of the most determined young ladies I know and extremely ambitious. She is beautiful inside and out and makes us laugh all the time.

After the boys proposed, the girls included me in every step of wedding planning. I never imagined I would get to go wedding dress shopping, schedule floral appointments, or go to cake and caterer tastings, yet I was able to do all of these things—twice!

Wedding dress shopping was my favorite. They looked like princesses in their gowns. There was a part of me that was sad as I thought about how I would never see my Ansley in a wedding dress, but mostly I was so very thankful the girls loved me enough to include me.

At Hannah and Austin's wedding, Hannah arranged for Robert to do a first look with her in her dress. She took mother-daughter pictures with me, and she and Austin added scriptures about rainbows into the ceremony.

At the reception, she surprised Robert with a father-daughter dance. Hannah's parents shared special moments with us that are typically reserved for the bride and her family. Through their thoughtfulness and selflessness, weddings have been redeemed for us. Weddings are beautiful to us again. We are so blessed and thankful for our Canadian family.

Kelsie is my girly girl. Whenever I need decorating advice, help picking out a new outfit, makeup rescue, or just need cheering up, I call Kelsie. She and I have bonded so much over these things, but my favorite bond we share is our love of gardening.

2023 was our year to experiment with planting and growing produce. We swapped ideas and pictures. There is something so satisfying about growing something from a tiny seed. You water it, care for it, clear out the weeds, and eventually it produces a harvest. I see our relationship like that. What we share is beautiful.

I love our conversations and the love we share, but most of all, I love that she calls me Mama Nancy. When I need cheering up, I watch one of the videos she made with her goats about her crazy farm adventures. They always bring a smile to my face.

We first met the girls at our home on Sapphire Circle. We would play cards at the kitchen table, make adventurous desserts, and laugh at our Pinterest fails. Hannah and I loved to cook and bake, and Kelsie loved being our taste tester. We would curl up on the couch and watch a movie or talk about all the crazy funny names they would name my future grandchildren. We dreamed of all that was to come and became a true family. My family went from a party of four to a party of six.

The girls could never replace my Ansley, but they helped fill a void that existed for fourteen years. Through Kelsie and Hannah, the Lord restored what the enemy tried to steal from me. Those moments I used to dread or think I would never experience have been redeemed. I am so thankful for my unexpected rainbows and the beautiful daughters the Lord has given me.

Nancy with Hannah and Kelsie.

CHAPTER FIFTEEN

Guilt

Do you blame yourself for what happened to your child? Do you replay the events over and over in your mind praying the story will have a different ending? I know I did.

I blamed myself for Ansley's death. I did not tell anyone I felt responsible—not my husband, my parents, my counselor, or my best friend—no one. I was too ashamed.

We had spent all summer at the hospital, and when they finally offered to let me bring her home, I jumped at the chance. I would have done anything to get her out of there but coming home proved to be a much more difficult task than expected. I was a Registered Nurse, but I was a mother first, and I was not a trained intensive care unit (ICU) nurse.

Ansley was on numerous IV medications I administered to her via a CADD pump. She was also on oral meds she received through her naso-gastric (NG) tube, in addition to food. In the nursing field, we call her condition "total care." The meds ended after midnight and started back up before 6 a.m. I was exhausted. I did not trust anyone to help me, and I wore myself down.

In the middle of one night, Ansley spit up her food all over herself and her bedding. I had only slept a couple of hours, at most. I was irritated as I walked into her room. Without thinking, I pulled out her NG tube and took her to my husband. I handed her to him saying, "Take her before I hurt her." He took her and just looked at me, not saying anything. I was so ashamed, but I felt as if I were losing control. I was emotionally and physically exhausted. My memories of that night formed the foundation of the pit of guilt I started digging myself into.

The morning of Ansley's last day on earth, she was burning up with fever. I called and made her an appointment with the pediatrician. She took one look at Ansley and asked which hospital we used. I broke down in tears.

"Please do not make me go back there," I begged.

She looked at me and said, "Ansley will get better care at home." The doctor trusted me. She told me to call the home health nurse and have her come out to put the NG tube back in. She also ordered a nebulizer for the house.

After Ansley passed, all I could think about was how could I not take her to the hospital. What was I thinking saying I did not want to go back to the hospital? If I had taken her in, maybe she would be alive right now.

After I gave Ansley her first breathing treatment, I knew something was wrong. She had an unnatural, rhythmic cry. I changed her diaper and paced the room. I knew she was in trouble. I blew air into her mouth and realized I was about to have to perform CPR on her. I ran to my neighbors. I told my neighbor I needed to get Ansley to an ambulance quickly. I was beginning to panic.

Why didn't I just call 911? Perhaps they could have gotten to us faster than we made it to them. What was I doing blowing into her mouth? I know how to perform CPR. Where had all my training gone?

I was diving deeper and deeper into my pit of guilt.

For years, 11 years to be exact, I allowed Satan to whisper all of the "what ifs" into my mind. I did not realize guilt could be demonic. I did not feel I deserved to be happy after all the mistakes I made. I did not realize the oppression I was living under.

In 2012, our marriage was struggling and we sought help. We went to a Christian counselor who was finally able to get me to open up. I had not been to visit Ansley's grave since 2002. The counselor asked me why.

"It is my fault Ansley died."

My husband looked at me shocked, shaking his head. "No, Nancy. No."

I knew he would never understand how I felt, which is why I never voiced it. Our counselor labeled my guilt for what it was, a lie from the devil. He pulled out his Bible and read something to me that changed my life.

"All the days ordained for me were written in your book before one of them came to be." The verse was Psalm 139:16. God knew Ansley before He formed her in my womb. He knew she would only be here for a short time. Her death was not my fault. I felt as if a cloud of sadness lifted from me.

The Word is truth, and it will set you free, but hearing that verse one time was not enough. I still must remind myself of the truth of that verse from time to time.

You will have to keep the Word constantly in front of you. I suggest writing scriptures on index cards and putting them where you can see them all over your home. Read the Word until it sinks deep within your heart and mind. Do whatever you need to do to get the truth into your heart, and the lies of the enemy out.

The devil likes to remind me of memories that lead to guilt. He wants me to return to the bondage he had wrapped me in for years. I have had to learn to do as the Bible says and take every thought captive. Sometimes, it is easier said than done, but I know Satan is a liar. He only comes to steal, kill, and destroy (John 10:10). In 1 Peter 5:8, the Bible says the devil is like a roaring lion, seeking someone to devour.

If you are experiencing any form of guilt over what happened to your child, do not hold it in. Satan wants to trap you in guilt, locking you up inside, away from everyone. Get help. Talk with your pastor, your spouse, or a trusted friend. If you need it, get professional counseling. There is no shame in seeking help. I met with a grief counselor for over a year, and I credit her with helping to save my life. I knew I could share anything with my counselor and there would be no judgment.

Father,

I pray the person reading this right now will receive the truth found in Your Word. You knew the days ordained for their child before they were ever born. Their death was not a surprise to you. In fact, You welcomed their child home with open arms.

Their child is whole, healthy, and happy. Help them hold onto the truth. Give them peace, Lord, that only You can give.

I ask this in Jesus' Name,

Amen.

Healing Hearts

Write out scriptures that remind you of God's truth and goodness.

CHAPTER SIXTEEN

Finding Joy in the Rainbows

by Robert Gearhart

When we lost Ansley, I thought about all the things I would miss: the dance lessons or sports games—probably both, birthdays, graduations, watching her fall in love, and being the proud daddy walking her down the aisle at her wedding, and dancing with her to the song *Butterfly Kisses* by Bob Carlisle.

It was not fair. The thoughts of loss consumed me and I did not want to go on. I became angry every time Butterfly Kisses came on the radio, or we heard it at a wedding. Most of the time, I would change the channel, but occasionally, I would listen to it sobbing. I was angry at God for taking Ansley.

I reluctantly went through a men's Christian retreat about five months after Ansley passed. At this point, I had nothing left to lose. The first night I was there, all I could think about was how badly I wanted to leave, but God had a plan.

On Friday, I listened as men gave their testimonies. Many of them had lost a child. God knew I needed to hear I was not alone. Other men have gone through this loss and survived. As part of my weekend, we had the opportunity to dedicate our children who had gone to be with Jesus.

It was not until Saturday evening that I fully submitted to the Lord. All weekend long, they played a song by Casting Crowns titled, "Who Am I?" I sat in the small chapel feeling alone, angry, and sad when they played the song "Who Am I?" again. I really listened to the lyrics this time.

"Who am I, that the Lord of all the earth would care to know my name? Would care to feel my hurt?"

For the first time in my life, I heard God speak in an audible voice.

"Robert she is with me, and you WILL see her again."

I broke. That was the moment I accepted the Lord Jesus Christ and dedicated my life to Him. He knows me. He cares for me. He knows what I am going through. It was an incredible feeling to embrace those truths.

The men I attended that weekend with showered me with love, prayer, and hugs. They were "Jesus with skin on," as we say in our family. There are times in our lives when we need someone to come alongside us and help carry our burden. I do not know where I would be today without them, and I am so thankful to call them friends to this day.

Life was not magically perfect after that weekend. I still wrestled with anger from time to time. As men, I think we often want to fix things. I wanted to fix the grief my wife experienced, but she would not let me.

I was hurting. She was hurting. My grief and frustration would often manifest as anger. I would take my emotions out on my boys and my wife.

I tell you this not out of a place of condemnation, but out of validation. I had to learn to rebuke the thoughts the devil whispered in my mind. I had to come against the false belief that "God did this to me."

The devil is a thief who comes to steal joy. I had to learn to hush the voice of the enemy and focus on what the Lord was saying. Sometimes He would speak through a song on the radio, through reading His Word, or by having someone call me. Other times, He would send me a rainbow.

It has been 22 years since we lost our Ansley. I miss her every day, but I know she is safe. I know who has her, and that even if she were given the chance to come back to us, she would choose Heaven. She is happy and whole, and I know one day I will see her again.

The Lord has restored so much in our family. We now have two beautiful daughter-in-loves. My wife is amazing. She has a heart of gold and loves Jesus. We are about to celebrate our 32nd wedding anniversary. We have a wonderful group of friends who would drop anything to come and pray with us. It does take a village to make it in this fallen world.

My prayer for you today is that you find people who will support you and pray for you. People that will be there when you're down. I tried doing it alone. I tried to fix my pain. It did not work.

In Matthew 11:28, the Lord tells us, "Come to me, all you who are weary and burdened, and I will give you rest."

Do not try to carry what you are feeling on your own. Lay it at the feet of Jesus. I leave you with this prayer found in Numbers 6:24-26, "The Lord bless you and keep you; the Lord make his face shine on you and be gracious to you; the Lord turn his face toward you and give you peace."

By the way, I did get the father-daughter dance I longed for. My daughter-in-love is from Canada. After she danced with her dad at her and my son's wedding reception, she held up a sign in front of me that read, "American Dad, will you please dance with your Canadian daughter?" I bawled like a baby. Everyone who knows me knows what a precious moment that was for me.

Robert dancing with his Canadian daughter-in-love, Hannah.

CHAPTER SEVENTEEN

Regret

Regret is a normal emotion of life. We can feel regret over something we should have done that we did not do. We can feel it over something we did that we should not have done. We can even feel regret for not knowing what to do at the time, and learning later what we could have done differently. We are all susceptible to regret.

Peter felt so much regret after he denied Christ that he wept bitterly (Luke 22:62). Judas felt regret after betraying Jesus and he tried to undo his actions by returning the blood money (Matthew 27:3-5). God does not want us to focus on regret. If we allow it, regret can consume us.

Instead, God wants us to focus on repentance. We need to lay our regrets at the feet of Jesus and leave them there. Let the Lord restore our souls and transform our lives.

Turning away from regret is easier said than done. You may need to lay your emotions at the feet of Jesus over and over again. I know I had to lay regret down multiple times.

I wish I could have those years back after Ansley passed. My greatest regret is knowing I missed special moments with my boys. At the time, I was depressed. I existed, but I was not emotionally present and living a full life.

I gained a tremendous amount of weight. I formed a literal barrier around myself to match the invisible one I had created. I wanted to keep everyone out.

I never wanted to hurt the way I did during those first six years again. My boys were six and eight years old when Ansley died. They were 12 and 14 before I finally came out of the oppression. I missed out on so much with them. My world was black and white during those years. I felt no joy, no hope, and no peace.

My boys changed because of who I became during that time, especially my Andrew. Andrew had always been a happy baby and child. He was goofy and quiet, but thoughtful and caring. When he realized that mentioning Ansley around me crippled me, he shut down. He never brought her up to me again.

Andrew would try to shush Austin when he would talk about Ansley. He was trying to protect me. My eight-year-old was trying to protect his mommy. It makes me sick to my stomach thinking about it even all these years later. Regret tells me I was such a bad mom, but I know the truth is I was doing the best I could.

God was so gracious. He sent Godly women into our lives to help fill the gaps I left. My mom, Melissa, and many others were there for my boys when I could not be.

I began to draw close to the Lord and ended up losing weight and starting to live again. I will never get those years with my boys back, but we have been making amazing memories since I have come back to life. We still are making good memories.

My boys are amazing inside and out. They married beautiful women of God and I am so proud of them. I pray they will forgive me for the times I was not there for them. I pray they will forgive me for putting them in a position where they felt they needed to protect me. I love them so very much.

As you read this chapter, what comes to mind? What do you regret? Are you willing to lay it at the foot of the cross? I challenge you to pray this prayer with me.

Lord,

I lay my regrets at Your feet once again and I pray those reading this will do the same. I cannot undo what has been done or do what was left undone. Help me to not focus on regrets but on restoration.

Restore our souls and breathe fresh life into us. Help us see our situations through Your eyes. Forgive us for not trusting in You and Your plan. Give us Your strength, Your comfort, and Your grace.

Thank you, Lord, for Your compassion, Your grace, and Your mercy.

Amen.

Healing Hearts

Do you have any regrets? Leave them at the cross, at the feet of Jesus.

CHAPTER EIGHTEEN

From Storms to Rainbows

by Andrew Gearhart

Growing up in a home after a tragic loss is not easy. It breaks everything normal and nothing goes back together the same. Losing my sister at four months old cast an unfathomable shadow over my family. The pain was compounded by the fact that my little brother had to be resuscitated a few years earlier, also from a heart issue.

Heart problems were not something I could grasp fully at that time. I knew it was not fair, and I knew it was not right. Aside from that, I knew nothing else. I was only eight years old at the time Ansley passed, and I did not know how to help or support my parents.

I avoided talking about Ansley or how I was feeling, as I could see it hurt my mom. I remember feeling a profound sense of helplessness because I did not know how to ease the grief my parents felt.

As the years passed, my daily routine revolved around school, homework, sports, and work. I was in school during the day, and spending time with my brother and neighbors at night. I played baseball and soccer, was on the swim team, and I loved skateboarding. On Wednesdays and Sundays, we were in church. I had a full schedule, and before long, I was off to college.

Shortly after I left for college, my mom started working on Ansley's Rainbows of Hope, an organization to help families like ours. I was proud of her for turning something traumatic into something positive that would help others. I would join her for board meetings and fundraising events when I had time, and it was good to see she was staying busy and pouring love into the families she served in their greatest time of need.

As my parents became empty nesters, they became more social. They went on trips, spent time with their friends, and volunteered at the church. It was great seeing them happy and learning how to navigate this new season of their lives. They found comfort in shared experiences and meaningful relationships with their friends.

A few years later, I met the woman who is now my wife, Kelsie. After a while, I invited her to one of Mom's fundraisers for Ansley's Rainbows of Hope. It was at the Mellow Mushroom where Kelsie and I were both working at the time.

My wife is funny, witty, and upbeat. She can take a joke and is always excited for an adventure. We spent a lot of time with my parents, going out to dinner, cooking meals at home, and going on trips. My dad loved to prank Kelsie and scare her or hide her shoes. It was sort of a rite of passage into our family. He was having fun and just being his goofy self.

I began to see my mom's spirit lift. She would become inspired and excited to plan trips for all of us. I watched her find purpose again. Our family was healing, and my parents were finding a new normal. We were having fun again, in a different way than before, but in some ways, it was better than before.

I know there are things my parents always wanted out of having a daughter, and I like to think my wife and my brother's wife helped fill the emptiness they felt for so long. Everyone processes grief differently. I honestly didn't know what it was like for my mom, but I can tell you this, I did not grow up comparing her to other parents.

My parents are hard on themselves over what they feel they should have done differently, but I am not. I do not reflect on who they were. I care more about who they are today and who they choose to be.

I believe the best thing we can all do for each other is to love and respect one another. I am proud of who my parents strive to be, and I am proud of their courage to do the reflective work it takes to grow and move forward after grief changed their lives.

I'm thankful for the love and support they give me and my wife, and I look forward to any time I get to spend with them, especially when the whole family can get together.

My prayer for you as you walk through this time is that you find strength in the Lord to get up each day and remain rooted in Him. Grief is no easy storm to navigate, but I know through God, your family, and your friends, you will start to find small happy moments, and healing will come in time.

Your rainbows will come. Know that although we have felt pain here on earth, it is meant to strengthen our faith, so we can spend eternity with the ones we love. I pray you take each day step-by-step and cherish the ones around you.

". . . Now is your time of grief, but I will see you again and no one will take away your joy." John 16:22

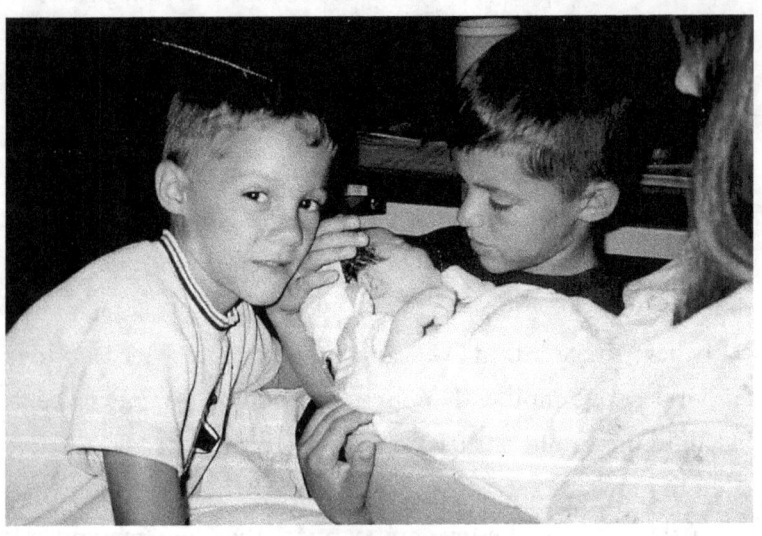

Andrew holds Ansley as Austin looks at the camera.

Kelsie, Robert, and Andrew at Yelllowstone National Park.

Andrew, Kelsie, Robert, and Nancy at Christmas.

CHAPTER NINETEEN

Permission to Hurt

There are three days a year I dread: Ansley's birthday, the day she went to be with Jesus, and Mother's Day. In the beginning, each of these days was equally painful, but her death anniversary soon became the one I dreaded the most.

The days leading up to the anniversary date were especially torturous. I tortured myself, or I let the devil torture me. I would replay the events over and over again in my mind, remembering every detail, every regret, and every mistake I made. The memories were so vivid, the feelings so real.

I could smell the hospital all around me. I could feel a sense of doom looming over me. Breathing became laborious. Panic attacks were more common during that time. Tears would fall without me even knowing I was crying. I was sad and brokenhearted. I wanted to spend time in bed, but I had to work, so I would grieve at work.

As the years rolled by, each anniversary became a bit more bearable. Twenty-two years later, I can tell you I still remember everything. I still hurt. I still cry some, but overall, I can go on living. I remember Ansley, but I choose to remember the good and not dwell in the sadness.

I often listen to sermons by Joyce Meyer while I am getting ready for work in the mornings. One of the things I learned from her is to, "trust God and do good." On difficult days, I look for rainbows. I pray for a family I can bless through Ansley's Rainbows of Hope. I believe and trust God is good and His plans are much better than ours.

But, you know what? It is okay to be sad. It is okay to miss your loved one. It is okay if you need to take a mental health day. Give yourself permission to feel how you feel. Recently, my husband and I were picking out flowers for Ansley's grave for Christmas. I stood in the aisle and started to cry. All of the flowers reminded me of old people. Where are the flowers that look like they are for a child's grave?

My husband took me in his arms and started picking out flowers that would work. I still hate having to shop for flowers for my daughter's grave. I am finally at a place where I can allow myself to feel angry and to feel sad about it, but now I move on more quickly.

I can remember a time when I felt guilty about smiling or laughing. I felt guilty if I felt any kind of happiness or joy. I worried about what others thought.

Did they think I was okay? I was not.

Did they think I no longer missed her? I did.

Did they think I was over being sad? No way.

I know now the feelings of guilt and regret came from the enemy of my soul. He kept me bound by fear, memories, and other negative or sad thoughts. I am angry at myself for letting Satan control me the way he did.

When I think of all the moments I missed with my boys, I feel sick. I missed making memories I will never make. Those moments that are lost forever. I am so thankful God restored me.

Once I realized Ansley went home in His timing, I was set free from all the guilt and regret. I allowed myself to feel happy, to feel joy, to give and receive love.

We started to make new memories as a family and have grown stronger and closer because of all we had survived together. I pray that you do not go through what I went through, but if you do, recognize it for what it is. Feeling sad is normal, but don't let Satan oppress you, or keep you from living the full life God has for you.

Your trigger days will, most likely, not be the same as mine. You may not have any at all, or you may have more triggers than I did. You will survive. Grief feels very intense in the beginning but give it time.

I challenge you to do something you enjoy today or this week. Make a memory with your surviving children, your spouse, or someone close to you. It is okay to feel happy. It is okay to smile, and it is okay to laugh.

As bad as things feel and look right now, there is always something to be thankful for. Make a list of the things you are grateful for and thank God for them. You will be surprised how an exercise in thankfulness can help you heal. Put on some praise music and praise Jesus. There is no greater weapon against the enemy than worshipping God!

Lord,

You are our Deliverer. We bind up any attack of the enemy in Jesus' Name. Fiery darts will fall to the ground.

I pray for a hedge of protection around everyone who reads these words. I pray they will seek You first with all their heart, mind, and strength.

Give comfort and remind them they are not alone. The joy in their hearts is from You. I pray they will let peace and joy flow freely.

We praise you, Lord, for who You are and all You do for us. We love You so very much.

Amen

I wanted to include the lyrics to a song that brought me so much comfort. The song is "Praise You in This Storm" by Casting Crowns. I pray it blesses you as much as it does me.

This song is a reminder that God is sovereign. His plans are perfect and there is a reason why all our prayers are not answered. We may not get answers on this earth, but we can trust God is good. He never leaves our side, even in the middle of a storm.

Praise You in This Storm

I was sure by now, God you would have reached down
And wiped our tears away,
Stepped in and saved the day.
But once again, I say amen
That it's still raining
As the thunder rolls
I barely hear your whisper through the rain
I'm with you
And as your mercy falls
I raise my hands and praise
The God who gives and takes away

[chorus]
And I'll praise you in this storm
And I will lift my hands
That you are who you are
No matter where I am
And every tear I've cried
You hold in your hand
You never left my side
And though my heart is torn
I will praise you in this storm

I remember when I stumbled in the wind
You heard my cry you raised me up again
My strength is almost gone how can I carry on
If I can't find you
As the thunder rolls
I barely hear you whisper through the rain
I'm with you
And as your mercy falls
I raise my hands and praise
The God who gives and takes away

[chorus]

I lift my eyes unto the hills
Where does my help come from?
My help comes from the Lord
The maker of heaven and earth
I lift my eyes unto the hills
Where does my help come from?
My help comes from the Lord
The maker of heaven and earth

[chorus]

And though my heart is torn
I will praise you in this storm

Songwriters: John Mark Hall / Bernie Herms
Praise You In This Storm lyrics © Sony/ATV Music Publishing LLC, Warner/Chappell Music, Inc, Essential Music Publishing, Capitol Christian Music Group

Healing Hearts

Make a list of things you are thankful for. Make plans to make a new memory with someone you love.

T H A N K F U L

CHAPTER TWENTY

Rainbows for Grandmothers

by Lynn Wilson

I did not think anything could match the love I have for my children, but then I became a grandmother. My name is Lynn, and I am Nancy's mom. I still remember the day my oldest grandson, Andrew, was born.

I stood outside of the nursery window just beaming inside and out. A lady came to stand beside me and said, "It must be your first." I thought my heart would burst from the love I felt for our tiny bundle.

Andrew and I had such a special bond. Nancy and Robert would let him come spend a week here and there with us when we lived outside of Atlanta. Everything Andrew did was picture-worthy! He was such a good baby. He was always smiling, and he loved being with us.

When our Austin was born, my heart grew even more. I had two grandbabies to love on! We found out the day after he was born that there was something wrong with his heart. Our Austie, as we love to call him, was flown by helicopter to the hospital in Augusta. I kept Andrew so Nancy and Robert could be with Austin.

I could not stand being without them, so we loaded everyone up and met them there. Nancy explained Austin's heart defect and the surgery he would have. Our world was shaken to its core. As you have already read, our Austie is doing very well now. He is our miracle baby, and we are all so proud of him.

When we found out Nancy was having a baby girl in 2001, we were so excited! I bought her a pink robe and we got to work on creating the perfect nursery for her. Of course, we did not rest easy until Nancy had a special ultrasound to check the baby's heart; they said it was perfect!

As a mother, you want the best for your children. You wish them a life free of pain and full of success, joy, and love. You expect your children, and especially your grandchildren, to outlive you. You are prepared to go first, but when the unimaginable happens and they go first, it is devastating.

When we lost my granddaughter, the pain I felt was overwhelming. I felt pain not only from losing our precious Ansley but also from watching my daughter and her family grieve.

I did not know the right thing to say or do. The only thing I knew to do was be there for Nancy and help with Ansley's brothers. It was hard because Nancy's dad and I were grieving as well. We took life one day at a time, as best we could.

In 2013, Nancy asked if I could make a quilt using Ansley's bedding and blankets. I worked for months trying to make it perfect. It was pink and frilly, and I was so happy to finally feel I was doing something to help my daughter.

Grammy Lynn holding Ansley.

That Christmas, the quilt was the last gift she opened. I felt such a sense of excitement and anticipation as she opened the box. Tears filled her eyes as she pulled the quilt from the gift box, and I knew all the time and effort were worth it. Nancy told me that it was the most special gift she had ever received.

Nancy looks at the quilt her mother made out of Ansley's blankets.

In 2014, I had the honor of helping Nancy form Ansley's Rainbows of Hope. She knew she wanted to help families that were experiencing financial hardships when their child became critically ill. Lodging, food, and gas are so expensive, not to mention the medical expense that goes along with having a sick child. Nancy and Robert had experienced it all firsthand. The mental strain on families worrying about their children was enough without them having to worry about where their next meal was coming from.

Nancy started researching online about how to start a nonprofit and quickly became overwhelmed. I became a paralegal the year Ansley was born, so she called me for advice. I had started nonprofits with the attorney I worked for and was able to help guide Nancy through the complex process of forming a nonprofit.

The first decision Nancy had to make to start the nonprofit, was to decide the name. The Lord had used rainbows over and over again to provide comfort to her. Rainbows are a sign of hope from God to Nancy, so she chose Ansley's Rainbows of Hope as the name of the ministry.

The process of forming a non-profit took months. Filing for 501c3 status requires proof of everything and is very extensive, but we got it all prepared and it was approved on our first filing, which was a miracle in and of itself!

Attending my daughter's first board meeting for Ansley's Rainbows of Hope was one of my proudest moments. She was so eager to bless families like hers, and I could see how much joy was in her heart.

She started fundraising and began getting referrals. Local businesses and friends were donating and everything was falling into place. Not only did she help the families she served financially, but she met with them and gave them a gift bag. She loved on them and prayed for them. It is through helping others that I saw my daughter truly begin to heal.

Having to navigate grief is never easy. There are no words you can offer that will bring healing to your grieving child. In my experience, just being there and doing what I could to help with daily responsibilities was what was needed. Listening and not trying to fix things is also important.

When your grieving child asks for help, do what you can to help, but do not forget to allow yourself time to grieve. Your loss is just as important. Seek counsel if you need to; there is no shame in asking for help. If you do not take care of yourself, you will be unable to help your child.

In my now 75 years of life, I have learned that no matter the trial, there is always a rainbow on the other side. I sincerely pray you will find hope as you read how our family survived the loss of our Ansley. May God's blessings be with each of you, and may you find peace as you navigate your loss.

Sincerely, Nancy's Mom,

Lynn

CHAPTER
TWENTY-ONE

It's Okay to Feel Joy

I remember feeling guilty every time I smiled, laughed, or felt any sense of joy after our daughter passed. I felt as if feeling any positive emotion meant I was "getting over" her loss, or that I was forgetting her and moving on.

Sorrow and sadness had become my constant companions; I was comfortable with them. I felt so much guilt over her passing I believed I did not deserve any joy. I spent years in a gray fog. I would fake a smile when out in public. I would do my best to show excitement as my boys opened their Christmas gifts. All the while, I felt dead inside.

The sad thing is, I did not want to feel any better. I was the one who had pulled out her NG tube in the middle of the night and fed her with a bottle. I was the one who ran with her to my neighbor's when she went into respiratory distress instead of calling 9-1-1. I believed I did everything wrong, and the devil reminded me of that every moment of every day.

It took eleven years for me to find hope. The day the counselor pointed out the scripture Psalms 139:16 changed my thoughts forever.

All the days ordained for me were written in your book before one of them came to be. Psalm 139:16.

Yes, I could have handled the day she passed differently, but I know the outcome would have been the same. Her heart was sick. She was with us for four months, and I can honestly say she transformed our lives. I know with everything in me, God sent her to save us. We would never have sought after the Lord had we not gone through what we went through. I would not be writing this book had we not lost a child.

I pray your situation is completely different from mine, but I believe most of us who have lost a child feel some guilt about feeling joy, at least in the beginning.

It is okay.

Your joy, your happiness, even your grief, is a testament to your love. Allow yourself to feel how you feel in the moment.

Don't let the lies of our enemy plague your thoughts. The devil knows the longer he can wrap us up in bondage, the longer we are ineffective for the Kingdom of God.

I know I say this a lot but give yourself grace. Be sad when you need to be, but know it is okay to laugh when your friend, spouse, or family member does something silly. Your child in Heaven is laughing with you.

Lord,

We need your joy more than ever. Remind our souls that even though we feel a deep sadness, Your joy can be present. Feeling joy does not mean we love our lost child any less, it means we love You more.

Thank You for your mercy and your grace. Thank You for loving on us even when we do not recognize it is You doing it. Wrap Your arms around the grieving loved ones, Lord. If they do not know You, I pray they seek You now.

In Jesus' Name, Amen.

Healing Hearts

Write down a memory that brings a smile to your face.

CHAPTER TWENTY-TWO

Sapphire Rainbows

by Kelsie Gearhart

I met Nancy's son, Andrew—whom I call Andy, when I was 19 years old. As our relationship began to progress, I remember finding his family so striking. I had seen pictures and videos on Facebook of his family. From that, I saw they had smiling faces, lots of friends, and a family that was social and busy. They looked like they had so much fun. His parents constantly surrounded themselves with friends and went on trips.

It was almost a year before Andrew introduced me to his parents. About six months into us dating, before I met his parents, I started to dream about Andy's mom. It was happening almost every night. I would wake up crying from these dreams. I felt so strongly I was meant to know her. In my bones, I was certain God wanted me in her life.

I knew from Andy that his mom had lost a child, a little girl, and it had happened 13 years ago. It wasn't something he ever really spoke of. I didn't think much of it, nor did I link my dreams about his mom to the loss of Ansley.

Grief was not something I had ever experienced. At my age, I couldn't fathom being plagued by something for more than a few weeks at most. After seeing the photos Andy shared of his family, I wouldn't have thought grief was anywhere near them.

I remember thinking his mom could experience a lot of mother-daughter things she missed out on with me—if she wanted to. I longed to be part of their family.

My intentions were good. I wanted to help Nancy heal. I wish I had realized I needed to set my expectations aside and meet her where she was.

I had months to dream about the things I wanted to experience in a daughter-role with Nancy, but she had just met me. I was hurt when she did not return the same interest in me.

Looking back I can understand, but at the time I was devastated. I wish she had handled things differently. I would bring up Ansley and wondered what she would be like today. I felt rejected when Nancy didn't want to talk about it. I now realize she was not ready to have that conversation with me.

Nancy and I both made mistakes in those early years, but God is a God of restoration. It is not easy coming into a family who has suffered a great loss. I do not have all the answers. I wish I had asked Andrew more questions.

I'd like to share a few things I've learned from my experience. I learned I cannot change someone else's past. I cannot heal their broken heart, but I can be there for them.

If you are like me, trying to build relationships with people who are grieving, I would like to share some advice. First of all, be open and let them know you are there if they ever need to talk.

Do your best to not to take things personally. Just because the other person may get up from the dinner table in tears, does not mean they are angry with you. Triggers can pop up at the most unexpected times.

Be soft, warm, and patient. Pray for wisdom and grace. Love the person who is hurting where they are. I would also suggest reading a bit about grief. Hopefully, reading this book is opening your eyes to the heart of a grieving mother.

For the grieving family I'd like to say, be graceful when someone who does not really know you has those "foot-in-the-mouth" moments. I did not realize I was saying anything hurtful. I never said anything out of malice. I just didn't understand the pain.

Communicate with your friend and family member as best as you can. If you are not ready to talk about something, just say something like, "Can we talk about that at another time?"

My mother-in-love, Nancy once said, "Grieving is not a free pass for rudeness." She told me she deeply regrets how she responded to me sometimes. We both hurt each other, and we didn't even mean to.

If you need space, ask for it. Too much talking too soon can be overwhelming. Love covers a multitude of sin (1 Peter 4:8). Let others love you, and try to love others as best you can.

Our early struggles made our family even stronger, but it wasn't all a struggle. We had a lot of good times. We have so many happy memories at their home on Sapphire Circle in Guyton, Georgia. Dinners, making fancy desserts and cracking up at our failures, playing card games, watching movies, going to church, picnics in the park, getting lost in a corn maze and so much more.

When Austin's girlfriend, Hannah, flew in from Canada for the first time we did all our usual things, but it was even more fun with her there. We all got along remarkably well. It was so natural and easy.

Hannah moved to Georgia and the routine continued. We bought matching family pajamas and did face masks together. We all even went on vacations together. I joked and called us all "the unit." Everyone loved that!

We had our first Christmas as a "unit" and Hannah and I both, totally unplanned, had custom gifts made that honored the family. I had a necklace made with everyone's birthstones, and Hannah had a custom art piece designed to showcase all the things Nancy and Robert loved. It was such a great surprise!

Looking back, it's spectacular to think that a woman who had been promised restoration by the One and Only was now at her kitchen table every night, surrounded by 20-something-year-olds who were making dinner, laughing, and playing card games with her. All of us were choosing her every single night. It wasn't forced; it was completely natural, a God-thing.

Nancy and Robert's table was full. Their home was full. Their hearts were full. God always fulfills his promises. I got to live through the days of us all at the kitchen table, roasting each other, cracking jokes, and making happy memories. I saw God gifting restoration with my own eyes.

Years later at Nancy and Robert's house in the mountains, I woke up in the middle of the night to a bright and bubbly voice that said, "Hi!" The voice pulled me out of deep sleep, and I had a vision.

In the vision, I could see the porcelain skin, massive brown eyes, and shiny long dark hair of a giggling teenager. I knew immediately it was Ansley. I can't even explain it. I just knew her, and she knew me. She was so happy and full of light! I was stunned—completely in awe.

Just as fast as that moment came, it was gone. I knew God was letting me see a glimmer of Ansley. It gave me such hope for the ever after. I got to bear witness to the fact that Ansley is with Robert and Nancy.

I know if Ansley were here, I would fully embrace the big sister role. Oh, how much I would love to hear about her day, her friends, and her interests. Andrew and I would secretly send her money when she overspent her paycheck, pick her up when she had a little too much fun out with her friends, and Andy would no doubt come to the rescue for any late-night calls where she stayed out too late and didn't want mom and dad to know. I can imagine us letting her hide out at our house when she needed a change of scenery.

While I wish so much that we could've experienced all of that with Ansley, I see God's hands all over this family. There are thousands of things God worked out that put us all in the right place at the right time to build these beautiful stories. I call all those times Sapphire Rainbows because we made so many amazing and redemptive memories at Robert and Nancy's house on Sapphire Circle.

Nowadays, Andrew and I live in Tennessee, but we frequently call and catch up with everyone. Our careers and interests have put us all over the map, but we still share a strong bond. Nancy and I talk about gardening, obsess over decorating, discuss politics, what Congress is doing these days, come up with creative ways to make money or save money, decide which waterfalls we want to explore, talk about what the stock market is doing, try new skincare products, and so much more. We have many inside jokes and references that only those in The Unit would understand.

Never before has Jeremiah 29:11 been so real to me. "For I know the plans I have for you, declares the Lord, plans to prosper you and not to harm you, plans to give you hope and a future."

I pray healing over you, dear reader, and your loved ones. I pray for a peace that surpasses all understanding. I pray your friends, family members, and loved ones have the gentleness and grace to give you love and support when you are hurting.

I pray you listen well. I pray God's glimmers are loud and obvious. I pray God reminds you that you are not forgotten. I pray for supernatural discernment and wisdom so your faith will remain strong in the darkest moments. I pray you will know you are not alone, and that joy comes in the morning.

I pray you have eyes to recognize God's promise as it comes to pass. I pray you are always reminded that the God of the mountain is also the God of the valley.

I pray all of this in Jesus' name. Amen.

Daughter-in-Love, Kelsie, with Mother-in-Love, Nancy.

CHAPTER TWENTY-THREE

Trust

Trust is a hard one for me. It is easy to trust the Lord when everything is going well in your life, but when your child dies, where does trust leave you? The definition of trust is a firm belief in the reliability, truth, ability, or strength of someone or something. In my mind, I knew God could heal my Ansley, but He chose not to. I could not wrap my head around how a good God would allow something like the death of my child to happen.

The Bible tells us repeatedly to trust the Lord, and that He never fails us, yet why did I feel as though He had failed me? How could I trust that God wanted only the best for me? That His plans were truly good after all I had lost?

I decided the only way for me to know if God is good or not, was to get to know Him. I began by reading the Word and doing devotions most days. I want to share two scriptures God kept leading me to.

I will repay you for the years the locusts have eaten; the great locust and the young locust, the other locusts and the locust swarm; my great army that I sent among you. You will have plenty to eat, until you are full, and you will praise the name of the Lord your God, who has worked wonders for you . . . Joel 2:25-26

You intended to harm me, but God intended it for good to accomplish what is now being done, the saving of many lives. Genesis 50:20

When I read Joel 2:25-26, it builds my faith that God has promised to restore what has been broken and change it into something amazing. He has a purpose for our pain. He will turn our pain into something beautiful.

In Isaiah 61, the Bible talks about the Lord "comfort[ing] all who mourn . . . bestow[ing] on them a crown of beauty instead of ashes, the oil of joy instead of mourning . . ."

Do I wish Ansley had never died? Absolutely! But let me tell you what I know. I know without a shadow of a doubt I would not be where I am now in my relationship with the Lord had I not gone through this. I would not be writing this book. I would not have started Ansley's Rainbows of Hope, and I would not be blessing families who have children who are critically ill.

The fact is there is evil in the world, and because of evil we have sickness and disease, and, yes, children die. God did not will for Ansley to be born with a congenital heart defect, but He used her short life to change me and bless others.

Another thing I realized is God does not view death as we do. Death is not the end in God's perspective; it is only the beginning. Death is the threshold over which God carries believers into the Kingdom.

Jesus overcame death through the resurrection, so death is nothing to be feared. Only God knows the day and time of our departure from this life, but when that happens our first step is into His arms. Our children are with Him. He is holding them closely.

I wish I could tell you that I have it all together now and that I trust God 100%, but that would be a lie. I still struggle, though not nearly as much as I did when Ansley first passed. The difference is now, no matter what I feel in my emotions, I know, that I know, that I know, God is good.

Let's try to change our perspective to see death as the Lord sees it—as the gateway to eternal life. The only way we can think as God does is to use the Bible as the only lens through which we view the world and our circumstances. If you view Heaven the way the Lord does, He was doing our children a beautiful thing by welcoming them home.

As you reflect on what it means to trust, search the Word for scriptures about trusting God. Surrender your pain to the Lord. When you find yourself thinking negatively, use the Bible as your lens, reframe using scriptures, and think of something positive. Pray for the Lord to reveal His plan for turning your situation into something beautiful. He will answer you. The answer may not be in your time, but when you are ready, He will answer. Be patient.

Father,

Thank you for being patient with me and with those reading this book right now, even when we doubt Your goodness. Teach us to trust You in all circumstances. Help us to surrender ourselves and our situations to You. Help us to replace negative thoughts with positive ones. Help us to wait patiently and expectantly for good things to happen. Speak to our spirits today, Lord. Remind us our children are safe with You.

In Jesus' Name,
Amen.

Healing Hearts

Search for scriptures on trust and write them in the spaces provided. What do you need to surrender to the Lord?

CHAPTER
TWENTY-FOUR

Rainbows from Canada

by Hannah Gearhart

Hey there, friend. My name is Hannah Gearhart. I am married to Austin, Robert and Nancy's youngest son. I'm going to share a little bit about our story, and some things I've learned from joining a family who has suffered great loss. Whether this applies to you or not, hopefully, it will provide a different perspective on grief. I'm writing as someone who came in as a stranger but is now part of the family.

To give a little background on myself, I grew up just outside of Vancouver, British Columbia, as my parent's only daughter with three boys after me. My childhood was unique in the best way. My parents were intentional with their parenting and sought to raise us to know and love the Lord. I will forever be grateful for them.

I was homeschooled my whole life, which allowed us to have a lot of adventures and travels, as well as participate in many sports and activities. I'm very blessed to be able to look back on my childhood with a lot of positive memories.

During my growing-up years, death wasn't a stranger. I lost half of my grandparents, a childhood friend, and my great-grandmother all before I became a teenager. I lost even more loved ones after that; however, I never lost someone who was a part of our immediate family. My mom used to always comment on how thankful she was that we were healthy children. I can honestly say I didn't understand the weight of that until later in life. Sometimes health is something we take for granted until it isn't there.

Currently, Austin and I have been married for five and a half years. We live in Billings, Montana, where I work as an operating room nurse, and he works as a police officer. The story of how I became a part of the Gearhart family starts back in 2015.

Austin and I met while attending a five-month program in Tyler, Texas, called Youth With A Mission (YWAM). Essentially, YWAM is a Christian missionary training school with campuses all over the world. I was barely 18 and he was 19. I had never had a boyfriend, and he never used to imagine himself getting married.

The program we went through was unique and intense. Our entire group became very close. Through different speakers and sessions, and opportunities to share our personal stories, we learned a lot about each other's past.

Austin is a very open person, and he would willingly talk about his past when it came to losing his sister, as well as some struggles he faced growing up. I watched as people prayed with him and helped heal some of the hurt and pain he lived with. It was truly beautiful to see him grow and begin healing areas of his life.

Toward the end of our program, we spent one month in Uganda doing mission work all over the country. Our entire team got to see the good, the bad, and the ugly as we battled jet lag and physical and emotional struggles and watched each other minister to both the old and young. Before our relationship ever officially started, we knew each other so deeply as friends.

During the five-month program, I had the opportunity to meet Austin's mom and older brother. I met his dad when they traveled from Georgia to visit. Before I met Nancy, I remember sitting on the porch of our classroom where Austin told me how his mom was in the process of starting a non-profit to help families who had children in the hospital.

Knowing about their story, I was blown away by her strength and heart to help others in her daughter's memory. When Austin introduced us, I was met with warmth and kindness. I felt she sought to know me even though I wasn't even dating her son yet. We learned we both had a lot in common, including our competitiveness. Neither of us liked to lose at the games we played.

When I met Austin's older brother, Andrew, I realized they were about as different as could be, but both of their personalities fit so well together. I admired their relationship. Austin was so touched when his brother surprised him in Texas. He even shed a tear or two. Andrew was quiet but easy to get along with, and he made the best cookies!

I met Austin's dad, Robert, toward to end of our program. He was warm, and generous, and made me laugh. We even got to introduce him to our favorite BBQ place, which was a blast. Needless to say, I was in awe of this amazing family who had suffered so much grief yet was such a blessing to be around.

Years later, Austin and I were attending college in Georgia together, but I was still unsure of what career path I wanted to take. Ansley's Rainbows of Hope had taken off and Austin and I would often go to the hospital to help his mom with families. I think what led me to pursue nursing was watching my future mother-in-law comfort families and bring a little bit of peace to the chaos they faced.

I knew she was a nurse and had spent a lot of time in hospitals between working and being there as a family member with Austin and Ansley. Nancy inspired me in every way. I just wanted to impact the world in some small way, similar to how she did.

Nursing was never really something I had considered as a career path. I had spent very little time in hospitals growing up. Before long, I found myself dedicating my time to studying, applying for, and finally graduating from nursing school. It was the hardest thing I've ever done, and I've never regretted it.

When I started thinking about what it's been like entering into a family that has suffered such a loss, I had to give it some thought. It's never been something I've sat down to think about. The more I thought about it, I realized there are a few pointers that might be helpful for someone who is in a similar situation. I will say, however, that everyone deals with grief and empathizing differently.

Here are a few things that have stood out from my perspective. I've tried to write in generalizations, so what I say can apply to many different situations, but I know you may live them out differently based on your personality and circumstances.

Be quick to listen and slow to speak.

This concept is not new. It comes from a pretty well-known Bible verse. "My dear brothers and sisters, take note of this: Everyone should be quick to listen, slow to speak, slow to become angry," James 1:19. Though most of us Christians have heard this verse, it is a practice I believe we too often forget.

The power of just sitting and offering your full attention to someone is oftentimes more healing than sharing well-meant encouragement or words of wisdom. I'll be honest, I always thought I was the worst when it came to being around someone struggling with grief or a hard situation. I felt like I never had the right words to say, or the ability to decipher how the person wanted to be comforted. I'm ashamed to say I would sometimes shy away from those situations out of fear of doing something to make it worse.

All of my fear recently came to a head when one of my best friends called me late at night right after finding out her dad suddenly passed away. I tell you what, sometimes there are no words to express the level of sympathy you feel for someone, especially someone so close to you. When she got back into town after the funeral, she asked if we could meet up to talk. Of course, I agreed, and we met for lunch.

During that conversation, I kept asking the Lord to give me the right words to say that would be encouraging to her. I kept feeling this stirring to just be still and listen, which is funny because listening has always been my default, though I most often thought of it as a downfall. Maybe I wasn't as bad at helping out a hurting person as I thought I was.

Of course, there are times to speak encouragement and interact in the conversation, but let's not underestimate the power of active listening. In addition to listening, ask questions if the situation calls for it. Asking questions can be a way to give the grieving person the ability to share more if they want to. I have found some people find healing in sharing memories of a loved one.

Meet them where they are at.

It may seem pretty obvious, but it's important to meet people where they are at. People move through grief on different timelines. From my experience, even some minor things can trigger days full of tears. Even though our world may keep moving forward, theirs may be on pause. If possible, and if they are willing, include them in events that may bring them joy.

Several years ago, when I was engaged and in the throes of wedding planning, I was honored to be able to involve both of Austin's parents in different aspects of the process and the wedding day.

My parents were so gracious to share special moments traditionally saved for the bride's family, and I am forever grateful. I got to get dressed in my wedding gown with both my mom and Nancy—my American mom—helping. We all had special photos taken, but perhaps the most heartfelt moment of all was surprising my American dad, Robert, by asking him to do a "father-daughter" dance with me. It will forever be one of my nearest and dearest memories. It means so much that both my dad and Robert were involved and that they were willing and excited to participate.

Under different circumstances or timing, it may have been a more difficult or painful thing to ask Nancy and Robert to be a part of my wedding day celebrations. It could have had a detrimental impact instead of a positive one, just depending on where they were in the grieving process. That is part of meeting them where they are.

As the ones coming into the grieving family, we need to put aside our expectations and thoughts of what we think they want or need and follow their lead. I've always found it's better to ask than to assume you know what is best for someone!

Be full of grace.

When I say be full of grace, you can apply it to whatever relationship you have with the grieving person. For me, my marriage comes to mind. My husband, Austin, lost a sibling, a baby sister he loved so much. Even though he was young and doesn't necessarily remember all the details, the impact of that life-changing event has taken its toll on him.

As a result of his whole family going through such a traumatic event, there are some areas of his childhood and growing up years that have been difficult to navigate and they've affected his adult life and marriage. We've had to work through a lot of hard things, but through the struggles of unpacking baggage in marriage, I've seen him grow exponentially as a man and a husband.

Some days, I felt like there was no more grace or forgiveness left in me. I wanted to yell, shut down, or just wallow in how "unfair" things were. And I'll be honest, there are times I did all of that. It's easy to place blame or let resentment build up in your heart.

Let me tell you, folks, the enemy is after your marriage—especially when he knows you love the Lord and are walking out the calling on your life and in your relationship. That's where grace comes in.

I was able to come beside Austin and help him work through a lot of his buried hurt and built-up walls. None of it was easy, and it required a lot of selflessness, but we are better people because of it.

God's grace to us is often described as undeserved favor. If our perfect Creator can give us favor that we could never deserve, who are we to not offer grace to others even when it's hard? Staying in constant prayer and asking God to help you see their heart instead of focusing on the pain that manifests is a game-changer. Loving someone who has gone through the loss of a family member is not always easy, but by God's mercy, it can be rewarding and beautiful.

I cannot imagine what my life would look like if God did not bring Austin and me together. My life changed for the better by knowing and loving the Gearharts as I do my own family. Their story has given me a greater understanding and love for those who have lost a loved one. I cannot wait to see the legacy the Lord brings forth from their family line because of their faithfulness to Him through this journey.

I pray God wraps His loving arms around you in whatever you are going through. If you are like me and are coming alongside someone who is hurt or grieving, I encourage you to seek God's wisdom through prayer and scripture. Finally, may God bless you, keep you, make His face shine upon you, and give you peace (Numbers 6:24-26).

"The Unit" - Hannah, Austin, Robert, Nancy, Andrew, and Kelsie.

CHAPTER TWENTY-FIVE

Perspective

When the shock of learning Ansley had a congenital heart defect wore off, I became angry. I was angry the perinatologist had missed her heart defect. We had numerous ultrasounds specifically looking at her heart, yet each time they said it was perfect. I was so upset with her diagnosis I even considered consulting a lawyer.

Looking back, I am now thankful the doctors missed the heart defect in the beginning. I know it sounds crazy but let me explain. Had they found the heart defect during an ultrasound, the remainder of my pregnancy would have been spent in misery. I would have been a nervous wreck, unable to enjoy any part of it. I would have missed out on a natural delivery surrounded by my family and friends. If they had known about her condition, they would have moved her to ICU immediately after birth, and I would not have been allowed to hold her right away.

Instead of knowing about her condition, I had nine months of thinking I was having a healthy baby girl. I painted her nursery walls Pepto Bismol pink, as my husband, Robert, called it, with a heart trim all the way around the room. Her room was perfect. I had so much fun picking out little girl baby clothes and choosing names with Robert.

Ansley's birth was like a dream. My best friend was my labor and delivery nurse. She worked all night taking care of me. She made sure I had the best room in the hospital complete with a huge closet so she could set up a cot and sleep in the closet while I labored the following day. When it came down to it, she was too excited to sleep and stayed up with me despite working through the night. Robert, my mom, and my sister stayed with me the whole day. Robert even cut the umbilical cord! I loved my obstetrician, and I was so blessed she was there for the delivery.

Ansley's godparents brought the boys up to see their new sister shortly after she was born. The boys crawled up on the bed with me mesmerized by Ansley. It was a picture-perfect day.

The next morning, my family came back to see Ansley. We had several hours together thinking she was healthy. I would not trade that time for anything in the world. These are the memories I will cherish for the rest of my days.

Learning to change my perspective has changed my life, but it did not happen overnight. I was bitter and angry for a long time. I was trapped in a sea of guilt and could not find my way out. It took me fully laying all the guilt down at the foot of the cross to begin to see from a new perspective.

Now, I always try to find God and good in every situation. I use the Bible as a lens to see my situation through. God was the reason the perinatologist missed her defect, and I am thankful. What good would have come from knowing?

Of course, I would have preferred she not have the defect at all, but that was not God's plan. I do not know why He allowed her to die after only four months with me, but my relationship with Him would not be where it is today had I not gone through losing her. His ways are higher than our ways.

I am learning to trust God more and more, and it is a very lengthy process. I spend time in His Word getting to know Him. I have learned His plans for me are good and He is good.

As you reflect on my story, I challenge you to shift your focus from yourself to focus on Jesus. Try looking at your situation through His eyes. When you focus on yourself, it is as if you are viewing your circumstance through a small tube, only seeing part of the picture, and missing all of the periphery. When you view things from the Lord's perspective, you get a glimpse of the larger picture. His view is higher and expands your frame of reference. The image you see not only includes your situation, but it shows all the people your life and story influences.

Nancy and her best friend, Melissa, worship God at Bell Mountain, Georgia.

Jesus endured the cross because He looked past the pain of the moment and focused on the joy set before Him. He looked at the bigger picture and how what He went through would impact all of eternity. He sees the end from the beginning.

In one of my favorite scriptures, Romans 8:28, the Bible promises ". . . in all things God works for the good of those who love Him, who have been called according to His purpose." The word does not say "some things." It says, "all things." God will turn your tragedy into something beautiful if you let Him. Try changing your perspective this week and see how your experience of life transforms.

Lord,

Thank you for Your life-giving Word and for loving us unconditionally. Thank You that You love us even when we are angry with You. The parents reading this book right now are hurting. Lord, please teach them to change their perspective, to look for You even in the darkest valleys.

I thank You for the healing that is taking place in their hearts. Comfort them and remind them they are not alone.

I ask this all in Your precious Name, Jesus.

Healing Hearts

Are you looking at life from God's perspective? Like the lens of a camera, we can focus in on the small details, or we can widen our view and try to see a bigger picture.

CHAPTER TWENTY-SIX

Rainbow Families

When I started Ansley's Rainbows of Hope in 2014, I had no idea the impact it would end up having on my life. I knew I wanted it to be more than just providing financial support to families with a critically ill child. I had been where those families were. I had a child who survived, and I had a child who did not. I could relate to them all.

I received my first referral in December of 2014. I was so excited when the nurse manager from the children's hospital in Savannah, Georgia called me. She said a mom had asked her to pray for her, and she immediately thought of me.

I was excited and a little nervous. My husband went with me to pick out some gifts for the little boy and his mom. We arrived at the hospital, and I hesitantly knocked on their door. We sat with the mom and little boy for at least an hour. Robert played with him, and I chatted with his mom. It felt right. Before we left, I prayed over the child.

Praying out loud was not something I was comfortable doing, but I felt the Holy Spirit nudge me and I obeyed. I wish I could bottle up the feeling that came over me as we stepped outside that hospital room. I knew, for the first time in my life, I was doing what the Lord called me to do. I was so full of joy I thought I would burst. So many of the families we have blessed through Ansley's Rainbows of Hope have become like family to us, but there are three I feel led to share more about with you. The first story is of little Christian.

Christian

On February 11, 2016, Christian and his family were relocating from Ohio to Florida. They were moving to be closer to family after the sudden death of Christian's daddy. Everything they owned was in the car. As they were traveling South on I-95, one of their tires blew out causing the driver to panic and lose control of the car. Christian's brother, sister, and mommy suffered many broken bones, but it was Christian who suffered a subdural hematoma, which is bleeding on the brain.

When I received the call from the Ronald McDonald House supervisor, he told me he had a family in desperate need of assistance. He explained Christian was critically ill and that his mom had no one with her. My daughter-in-love, Hannah, went with me to the hospital to meet with Christian's mommy. We sat in the family waiting room as she recalled the haunting experience. The only clothes she had were the ones the hospital gave her from the lost and found bin, so Hannah and I went shopping. We bought clothes and toiletries and headed back to the hospital.

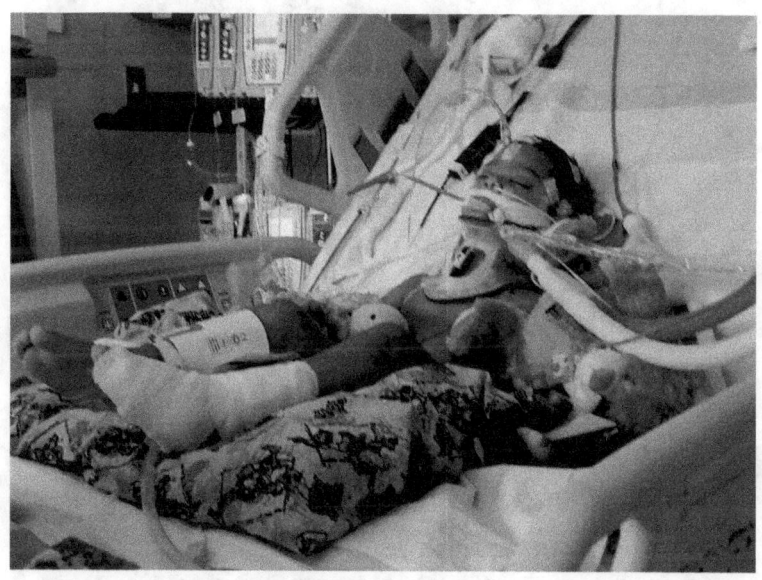

When we arrived, Christian's mommy took us back to see him. He was hooked up to so many machines. He had a slim chance of surviving, and even if he did, his head injury was so severe they did not expect him to walk, talk, or have any quality of life. We prayed over Christian and his mommy and visited them many times.

I can honestly tell you that I watched as God healed that little boy. Every single time we went to the hospital, I could see improvement. He began smiling, giving me a thumbs up, and saying short words. Before he was transferred to the hospital in

Atlanta for rehab, Robert and I took pizza to the hospital for one last visit. Christian crawled up into my lap and I just cried. I was holding a miracle.

Christian spent several months in Atlanta for extensive rehab. He had to relearn how to walk, talk, and eat. He was finally released to go home the next year.

He called me on video in 2021 and was cracking jokes and showing me all over his new home. He was so excited to tell me about school. To hear him talk and hear how well he is doing in school brought tears to my eyes. I think I cried the entire time we were talking. I was so very happy.

I have shared Christian's story many times. When I talk to him and his mommy, I remind them that the Lord has something very special in mind for Christian's life. He is going to do great things for the Kingdom of God. I am so thankful for the small part we were able to play, and especially for the opportunity to witness such a miracle.

Leena

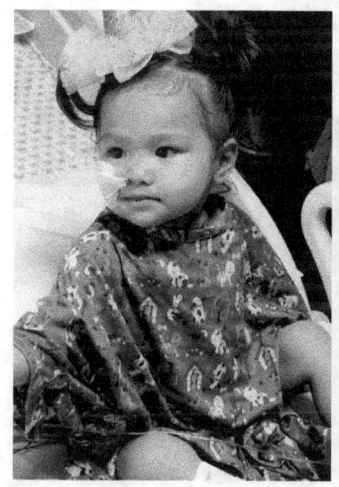
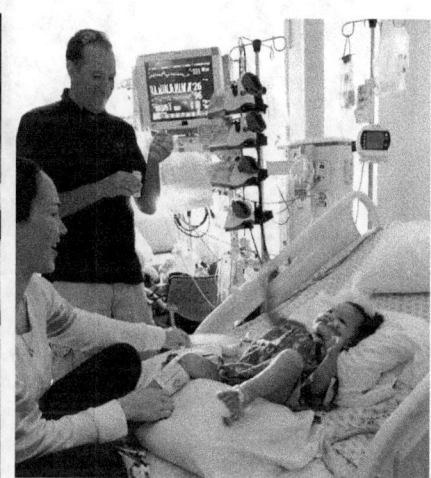

In May of 2016, my cousin told me about Leena. She had just turned two years old when she was diagnosed with cancer. She had a neuroblastoma growing in her belly. She went from being a bubbly little toddler to spending months on end in the hospital. Robert and I drove to Atlanta to meet with Leena and her Mommy. She was having a rough day, but when we pulled out some bubbles, she perked right up. Her weak smile melted our hearts.

Leena's mommy was still in shock. Their entire world had been turned upside down. We knew what that felt like.

Leena had multiple surgeries. She underwent a stem cell transplant that resulted in horrible side effects. She endured chemo and countless infections. She would bounce forward and then take ten steps backward. The rollercoaster of emotions her family went through was tormenting. When we learned she was in remission, I thanked God for another miracle.

There was just something about that little girl that made everyone who met her fall in love with her. I shared her journey on our Ansley's Rainbows of Hope Facebook page, and friends would often ask about her.

Leena had to undergo daily outpatient therapy in Jacksonville around Easter the following year. We were celebrating Easter at my parent's home in Brunswick, Georgia, and we invited them to join us. Her mommy made the hour drive north and they enjoyed a home-cooked meal. They both loved our Easter egg hunt. Seeing Leena open the basket the Easter Bunny brought her and watching her run around and be a toddler filled us with joy. It was such a special day, and one I am so thankful for.

When Leena's cancer returned, it returned with a vengeance. We were devastated. I remember the day I learned Leena had passed. My cousin texted me early on December 2, 2017 to give me the news.

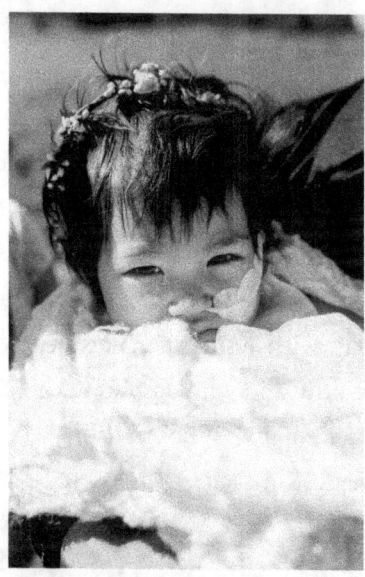

I cried for the precious child that was gone. I cried for the pain I knew her mother was experiencing. I cried there was nothing I could do to help them.

I was flying out to Arizona to meet Robert the next day. I had to see Leena's mom, so I drove to Atlanta. When her mommy came out of her room and saw me, she melted. I hugged her so tight; I did not want to let go.

There were no words I could offer that would ease her suffering. I just wanted her to know I was there. I went for myself as much as went for Leena's mommy. Sometimes you do not know what to do, but I knew just my being there would speak volumes.

Robert and I planned our trip home from Arizona so we could attend her funeral. I wanted to be there, but I knew it was going to bring up painful memories. As we walked into the funeral home, I saw Leena's mommy and family. I knew that look of despair. I understood trying to smile all the while wanting to run and hide. I hated they were going through this. I could feel their grief. It was not fair.

It has not been an easy road for Leena's parents, but they welcomed their rainbow baby the next year. They are learning to live again. They are learning how to be a family without Leena.

Leena forever impacted our lives. Her smile is a reminder that tomorrow is a gift. When I picture her running around with my Ansley, playing tag with Jesus, it makes my heart smile. Leena and Ansley are healthy and whole now. We helped Leena's family financially, but I believe it was the emotional connection we made that made the greatest impact.

Amen

In February 2019, I received a referral for a family whose daughter was born in Savannah and then flown to the Children's Hospital of Atlanta after being diagnosed with a serious heart defect. Amen was born with Ebstein's Anomaly of the Tricuspid Valve. Her doctors said it was one of the worst cases he had ever seen. She was in heart failure and was on ECMO (a heart and lung machine). Her condition was critical. Amen was just nine days old when we met her daddy.

I have a funny story about meeting Amen's family. The social worker had told me Amen's parents were recent immigrants from Ethiopia and shared that the family's primary language was Amharic. I decided to use Google Translate the first time

I reached out to her daddy via text. He texted me back saying, "You can text me in English." The Lord only knows what I ended up sending him!

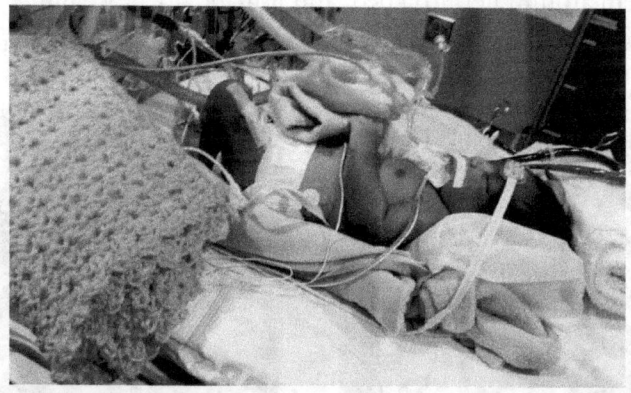

The social worker explained the family did not have a car, so we purchased a bus ticket to get her daddy home from the hospital in Atlanta so he could go back to work.

When we arrived at the hospital, the daddy took us into the intensive care unit to meet Amen. She had a head full of dark hair. She was so tiny and perfect. Robert drove her daddy to the bus station while I stayed with Amen. I prayed over her and held her tiny hand.

Amen suffered complication after complication, including a stroke. I cannot tell you the number of times we were told to pray. We were told more than once that the family had been called in because Amen was not expected to live. But God had other plans.

We visited Amen and her family in their home not long after she was discharged. Holding that baby in my arms gave me such joy and hope. God truly is a God that performs miracles still to this day.

One of my favorite blessings we have ever been a part of was arranging transportation for Amen's whole family to visit with her when she was in Atlanta. Her daddy sent me a picture of all of them around her little bed, and it made my heart smile. I was so thankful we could be a part of bringing the family together.

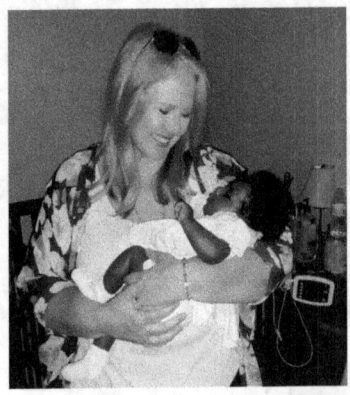

Amen is a walking testimony to that fact! She is now four years old and in pre-kindergarten! Her teachers brag about how well she is doing in school. When I think of how sick she was, and how she is today, I am in awe of the God I serve.

I could tell story after story of families that have impacted our lives. The families of Holland, Sophie, Trey, Sha'Riya, Brantley, John, Reid, Lachlan, Ky'Leigh, Magnolia, Syke, and Kendall, just to name a few, have touched us in ways they will never know. I have cried with families when their child passed and celebrated with those whose child recovered.

Spending time with the families Ansley's Rainbows of Hope serves and truly getting to know them has been one of the greatest joys of my life. They know I have walked in their shoes. Most feel comfortable sharing the good, the bad, and the ugly with me with no fear of judgment. I call these families my Ansley's Rainbows' families. Every time I get updates—sometimes months or years after we helped them—it is like an unexpected rainbow.

I am so thankful the Lord has turned my pain into purpose. I am so thankful for my Rainbow families.

CHAPTER
TWENTY-SEVEN

Triggers

Sometimes completely unrelated events can trigger a grief episode you were not expecting. I struggled with whether or not to share this story, but finally decided it was important. It's a recent experience of what we just went through with our dog, Bailey.

Bailey turned six in September of 2023. Now that our boys are grown, married, and busy with their own lives, Bailey and our other dog, Bentley, are like our children. They go just about everywhere with us.

We have tried breeding them for five years with no luck. This year, we decided to help the process along with artificial insemination, and it took. We were going to have grand puppies!

One week after the ultrasound confirmed the pregnancy, I noticed something was very wrong with Bailey. She was five weeks in, which is halfway to full term. I noticed she whimpered most of the day and began nesting.

I took her to the vet where I learned she not only had lost the pups, but she had a severe uterine infection called pyometra and would require an emergency spay. I was upset about the puppies, but my concern was for Bailey. I wanted them to do whatever they needed to do for her to be well. She had the surgery and suffered many complications that led to an overnight stay at the emergency animal hospital and a lot of medications.

I am very thankful to say that Bailey is well and back to her spoiled self, but the entire episode sent me into a depressed state. I do not know how to explain exactly how it made me feel. All my feelings of loss came back, flooding over me. Almost losing my sweet Bailey triggered my emotional memory.

I remembered not long after Ansley passed, I had an unnatural fear something was going to happen to my boys. I tried not to allow it to consume me, but it was always in the back of my mind. I did everything I could to allow the boys to live their lives without allowing my fear to infringe on their freedom.

When Andrew turned 16 and began to drive himself to school, I would follow him. He drove in the car in front of me, and I literally followed him. Yes, he knew I was there. I felt like if anything happened to him or Austin, I would die.

The thought of losing Bailey brought all of that old fear up to the surface in a very real and tangible way. The first several days of Bailey's recovery were rough. She was on seven medications, many were pills. She was refusing to eat so getting the pills down was traumatic both for her and for me. I cried a lot.

I felt myself slipping down the dark hallway of depression and was unsure of how to get out. I reached out to friends for prayer, and I forced myself to go outside. There is something about being out in nature, in God's creation, that helps me refocus. Every morning I would wake up and tell myself, "Today is going to be better," and it was. It was not an overnight healing, but it did come.

Loss is an inevitable part of life. Knowing that truth does not make it any easier. Loss hurts, some losses are worse than others. I don't want to think about losing my parents or a sibling; my heart cannot handle letting my mind go there. No matter how much I don't want to ever face loss again, I know that when it happens, God will be with me. I have learned the Lord is with me whether I am on the mountaintop or in the valley.

As I have been writing this book, I've prayed to be raw and authentic. It has been nearly twenty-two years since Ansley passed. One reason it has taken me so long to write is because it is painful taking myself back to relive that place of indescribable grief.

While speaking with a friend, I realized the Lord used the experience with Bailey to remind me of what my fear was like. Sometimes, the Lord will use an event to fulfill His plan. It was His plan for me to write this book, and to discuss every topic I've shared. He had to remind me of some of the things I felt back then, and He used a trigger to do it.

I know deep in my spirit that writing this book is part of my story. Had I not gone through what we just went through with Bailey, I would not have included this chapter. Had we not lost our daughter, I would not be writing this book at all. If this book helps just one person find hope in God through their most difficult times, it will be worth it all.

Robert and Bailey, Nancy and Bentley.

Lord,

When we have no words, lead us to Your Word. When we don't know what to pray, bring Your Word to our remembrance.

Your Word says when our hearts are overwhelmed, You are the Rock of Our Salvation (Psalm 61:2 and 95:1). Your Word says that when our hearts condemn us, You are greater than our hearts and You know all things (1 John 3:20).

We know that as You walked this Earth, You were a man of sorrows and well acquainted with grief (Isaiah 53:3). You did not shy away from tears or agony (John 11:35; Luke 22:44).

In this world, we will have trouble, but You have overcome the world (John 16:33). You came to heal the brokenhearted (Luke 4:18).

We believe You and thank You for healing our hearts, and for helping us to stand on Your Word during tumultuous triggers that try to drown us.

Thank You for stabilizing us emotionally, for helping us regain our footing when the waves of emotion knock us off balance. Thank You for Your grace and kindness, for never leaving us alone. Thank You for preparing a place for us in Heaven, and holding our hands as we walk toward Heaven every day.

In Jesus' Name, I receive spiritual and emotional healing. Amen.

Healing Hearts

The most important thing you can do to ground yourself after an emotional trigger is to speak the Word of God aloud. Look at the world around you. Your Creator made it all. He made you. He understands every emotion, and how to calm you.

Weather permitting, go outside and look around. Describe what you see, hear, smell, and feel. God's handiwork is all around us. Take a moment to soak it in. "The heavens declare the glory of God; the skies proclaim the work of his hands." Psalms 19:1

CHAPTER TWENTY-EIGHT

Rainbows that Bloom from Friendship

by Melissa Hunt

As a child, I always wanted a sister. That wish would not be granted to me until 1995 when I met Nancy in college. I like to say I chose her, but after almost thirty years, it's become abundantly clear that God put her in my path. She is my voice of reason, my greatest advocate, and isn't afraid to set me straight. After all, someone must! Her faith and her devotion to her family truly inspire me.

When Nancy and Robert found out they were expecting a baby girl, it was an unspoken fact she would have the whole world wrapped around her finger. Boy, were we right!

As a labor and delivery nurse, every birth is clear evidence of God's presence, and miracle to me. Ansley's delivery was extra special! We all cried at the unbelievably beautiful child with a mass of the softest dark hair you could imagine.

I got to place Ansley in Nancy's arms for the first time. Thinking of that moment still makes me cry tears of joy. I remember how my heart swelled with love, pride, and excitement in anticipation of our princess.

I remember when Andrew and Austin arrived to meet their baby sister for the first time. They were all smiles and bearing a gift: a tiny beanie baby for their tiny sister. They were so proud of her! As big brothers, we knew they would be her lifelong protectors.

Twenty-four hours later, the world stopped spinning as Nancy and her family went reeling into a world they hoped to never return to—ICU, cardiologists, heart surgeons. Then four months later, the unthinkable happened and all of our hearts broke.

Watching my best friend, her husband, and her boys ache as they did was so very painful for me. It left me feeling helpless. Nancy and I spent a lot of time together in the following months. I wanted to be able to say or do something to comfort her, but there was nothing I could do. Nothing can be said to make the pain of losing a child lessen. One thing I finally realized I could do was I could just *be* with them.

Sometimes, Nancy just needed me to come pick her up and get her out of the house. It was something I could do. My two-year-old, Sarah Rose, would be in the backseat with her hands in the air, singing and worshiping God, while also providing us some comic relief.

It was important for me to allow Nancy the opportunity to talk about how she was feeling, and to cry on her own schedule. It was all I could do to give her the space to feel bad sometimes or to feel normal. She needed me to be okay with whatever she needed to feel at the moment.

Ansley was a very bright light in our lives, and when we lost her, it seemed dark, as I suppose most losses do. Time, faith, and prayer won out as they always do.

For me, the light cannot help but come in when you know that one day, we WILL see Ansley again. Ansley changed my life; she changed me. She was only here for four short months, but her death pushed me toward God and strengthened my faith.

If you are walking beside a friend, "sister" or "brother" during their grief journey, just be yourself. Give her or him the grace to be themselves. There is no question that life is difficult but make the healing journey together.

I like to think that I helped Nancy through her most difficult time, but I know the truth is that in her deepest, darkest moments, she was helping me just as much.

2 Corinthians 1:3-5 reminds us that God comes alongside us when we go through hard times. Before you know it, He will bring us alongside someone else who is going through hard times so that we can be there for that person just as God was there for us.

Ansley's Rainbows of Hope was born of a broken heart to offer comfort and hope to those with a critically ill child. It is a reminder that God walks beside us when we are broken. My best friend's heart has been restored in walking alongside others.

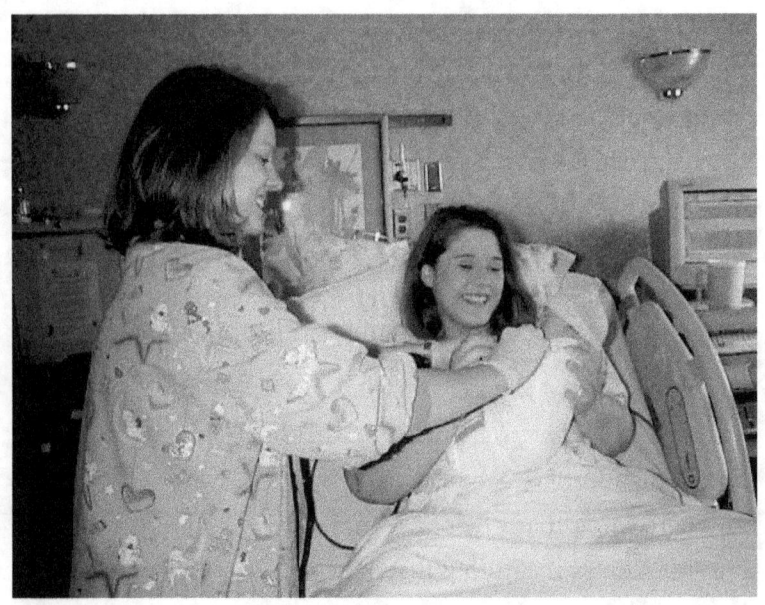
Melissa with Nancy and Ansley.

CHAPTER TWENTY-NINE

Marriage in the Rainbows

Marriage is not easy. Robert and I were 18 and 20 when we were married. Smart decision? Probably not, but God redeemed it. We had our first son, Andrew, two years after we married, and our son, Austin, not quite two years after that. We were a young military family. We made stupid decisions and a lot of mistakes, but we loved each other and our boys.

Losing Ansley after having her for just four short months rocked us to the core. We both knew of God, but we did not know Him. My grief was crippling. Robert would try to reach out, and I would push him away. I resented when he would dare to show his pain to me. That is hard to admit, much less write, even now.

I remember telling my grief counselor I needed Robert to leave. I could not take it any longer. My pain was killing me, and my perception was he was trying to dump his pain on top of mine. It was all just too much.

My counselor had Robert come in to meet with her, and then we started going together. I am so thankful for my grief counselor. I believe Jesus worked through her to save my marriage. I will be very candid and share that 2012 and 2022 were some of the worst points in our marriage. We were both ready to end it. It would have been so easy; uncontested divorces are not that costly, money-wise.

When we sat with a marriage counselor early in 2023, he concluded he had done all he could do. He felt it was best if we started to look at what life would look like for each of us apart. It hit me like a ton of bricks: after 31 years, it appeared our marriage was over. How did we get here? I could see the devil's handiwork all over the situation and in that moment something within me changed. I was not ready to give up, but I was not sure where to go from here.

The Sunday after that counseling session, Robert went to church to hear Pastor Jack at Southside Assembly. I was volunteering in the nursery at our home church in Pooler, Georgia. Robert texted me after church and asked me to meet him for lunch. He sat in the booth at the restaurant with tear-filled eyes and said he did not want our marriage to end.

He told me Pastor Jack said during the service that he had been praying all week for someone. He did not know who that person was, but that they felt like everything was over. They had given up. God wanted that person to know that they are not alone. He is with them right now. Robert took my hand and said, "That person was me."

No marriage on Earth is perfect. Social media paints a pretty picture, but no one posts the bad. Even if they do, it is one-sided, and only what they choose to share.

I have learned that surviving the death of a child puts things in perspective. It has given us something else to fight for. Why give up on our marriage now? We already made it through the worst time in our lives.

Robert and I are still working on our marriage. Communication is everything. We have become more intentional about praying together. We each acknowledge there is work we need to do in ourselves. For me, it is reading the Word. The Bible can bring hope and peace, but sometimes it brings correction. It will uncover sin and shine a light in the darkness. It is life-changing. I pray our marriage is a testament to perseverance and love, and that our struggles will help others push through their difficult times.

Marriage can be full of storms, but search for the rainbows. So often they appear after a terrible storm and we miss them. It is easy to focus on the negative. Sometimes it is necessary to be intentional and look up. Look for the signs of hope; look for the rainbows.

In December 2023, Robert and I celebrated our 32nd wedding anniversary. We are doing our best to navigate life as empty nesters. In the spring and summer months, you can find us racing down Lazaretto Creek with our puppies on our jet skis. In the fall, we are chasing waterfalls in North Georgia and watching the Georgia Bulldogs. In the winter, you can find us curled up in front of the fire place watching a movie or reading a book. I still practice as a nurse and love blessing families through Ansley's Rainbows of Hope. Robert hunts when he can, and is still involved with Tres Dias.

My oldest son, Andrew and his beautiful wife, Kelsie, bought their first home in Tennessee after graduating college. They are busy with work and running their mini farm. I have many grand pups, goats, chickens, and ducks. The rolling hills outside their front door are breathtaking.

Austin and Hannah, moved to Montana after graduating college. He recently graduated from the law enforcement academy there and is a police officer. He continues to see his cardiologist yearly, and my daughter-in-love always goes with him. Handing his care off to her was not easy for me, but because it was her, I knew he was in good hands. He is still not on any cardiac medications. They soak up every moment they can in the beautiful outdoors with my grand puppy, Dobby.

We do our best to get together as a family at least once a year, and we make the most of the time when we do. In 2023, we met in Montana for Austin's graduation and explored as much of Montana as time allowed. It was beautiful.

I am so thankful God has restored my family. Robert and I are still choosing each other every day. While no one prepares you for having adult children, we love this new chapter of our lives. There is nothing I love more than getting to spend time with my husband and our kiddos—all four of them!

Austin, Robert, Nancy, Kelsie, Andrew, and Hannah.

CHAPTER THIRTY

Rainbow Baby

Yesterday marked the 22nd anniversary of Ansley's homegoing. Grief is such a crazy thing. Even if I do not realize the date, my body instinctively knows. Around 3:45 in the morning, I awoke to the term "rainbow baby" echoing in my spirit. It seemed so random.

Later that morning, I Googled it. I had heard people say "rainbow baby" but didn't really know what it meant, and had never researched it. The definition that pulled up was ". . . a baby born after the parents have a pregnancy loss. The name draws on the symbol of the rainbow, representing beauty after a dark time."

Here I am, 22 years later, and the Lord is still reassuring me through rainbows! It stopped me in my tracks. Ansley was, in fact, a rainbow baby.

In 1999, I became pregnant with our third child, and we were thrilled. The boys were 4 and 6, and they were over the moon as well. We were sure the baby was a girl. We had started picking out names and wondering who she would be like. Would she be studious and quiet like Andrew, or wild and crazy like Austin?

Sadly, at my 16-week appointment, my obstetrician could not find a heartbeat. She tried multiple times and ways, but it was not there. I was alone when I found out our baby was gone.

You hear people talk about having miscarriages all the time. I had no idea how devastating it could be. We were crushed. I was too far along to let nature take its course, so the doctors admitted me to the hospital for a procedure. We mourned the loss of our baby.

The next year, in 2000, I became pregnant with Ansley. I don't think the term "rainbow baby" was around back then, and I honestly never recognized Ansley as being a rainbow baby, but she was! It is so amazing to me when I think that rainbows were a part of her life from the very beginning.

I'd like to share a passage of scripture that has always encouraged me. It is Isaiah 61:1-3.

> *The Spirit of the Sovereign Lord is on me, because the Lord has anointed me to proclaim good news to the poor. He has sent me to bind up the brokenhearted, to proclaim freedom for the captives and release from darkness for the prisoners, to proclaim the year of the Lord's favor and the day of vengeance of our God, to comfort all who mourn, and provide for those who grieve in Zion—to bestow on them a crown of beauty*

> *instead of ashes, the oil of joy instead of mourning, and a garment of praise instead of a spirit of despair. They will be called oaks of righteousness, a planting of the Lord for the display of his splendor.*

So much time has passed, yet the Lord is still blessing me with rainbows. I am in awe that the Lord who created the Heavens and Earth cares so much for me. He knows what a hard day October 24th is for me, and that very morning, He took the time to remind me He is right here with me.

Seeing Ansley in a new light, as my rainbow baby, was a confirmation to me that as hard as it has been reliving these painful memories as I write this book, God is with me. He truly is exchanging beauty for ashes, strength for fear, joy for mourning, and peace for despair. He is doing it for me, and He can do the same for you. He cares for you just as much as He does for me, and desires nothing more than to have a relationship with you.

Searching for Rainbows

I smile every time I see a rainbow. Often it is after a storm, but my favorite rainbows are when there is not a cloud in sight, and I spot a tiny one up in the sky. They are my reminder that I will see my baby girl again, that she is playing in Heaven with her sibling, and that my Lord and Savior is caring for my children.

I pray this little book has impacted your life and provided you with the hope you need to carry on. If you do not have a "rainbow" from Heaven of your own, pray and ask the Lord to send you some sort of sign. My rainbows bring me such joy, peace, and hope. I know having your own sign from Heaven would bless you as well.

If you are reading this and you do not know Jesus, I invite you now to pray with me.

Lord,

I cannot go through this life without You. I need Your forgiveness, Your hope, Your love, Your direction. I believe that You are the Son of God, and that You died on the cross and rose again.

Come into my life and be my Lord. Teach me Your ways. Fill me with Your Holy Spirit. Fill me with peace that passes all understanding.

Amen

Accepting Christ will not automatically make your grief disappear. Living for God will not mean you will not experience trials in this world. Knowing God and having a close relationship with Him will bring you hope, and it will determine where you will spend eternity.

Without Jesus, there is no other way to continue living a full life after losing a child. You can exist, yes, but not truly live. We need the blood of Jesus, the hope of Heaven, and eternal life.

My family is as healed as I think is possible on this side of Heaven from the loss of our Ansley. I still have my moments of grief, but I can push through now. I have learned that walking outside and changing my scenery can shift my perspective onto the Lord, and off of my feelings. Spending time with someone I love or helping someone in need is also a huge help.

Thank you for taking them time to read our story, and to share in our grief. In whatever you are going through, you are not alone. I am praying for you, and I would love to hear from you. In the meantime, I will continue searching for rainbows, and I pray you will as well.

God bless,

Nancy

SUPPORT

Support Ansley's Rainbows of Hope

From the time of its inception, until the publishing of this book at the end of 2023, Ansley's Rainbows of Hope has given over $100,000 in cafeteria gift cards, gas gifts, lodging expenses, and other travel-related expenses to families of critically ill children. On average, 94% of every dollar donated goes directly to the families we serve. We could not have blessed the over 300 families we have helped so far without the generous support of our donors.

If you have been blessed by reading our story and would like to give to Ansley's Rainbows of Hope, you can do so by mailing a check to the address on our website, or clicking the "Support Us Today" tab on the website.

www.ansleysrainbows.org

You can also donate via Venmo or Zelle.

@AnsleysRainbowsOfHope   Nancy@AnsleysRainbows.org

One-time donations are welcomed, and no amount is too small. You can also set up recurring donations. In addition, many companies offer payroll deductions as a convenient way to support your chosen charity. We thank you from the bottom of our hearts for choosing to support our mission and vision.

Our Mission

Having experienced the devastation of two of our children being born with heart defects and then spending countless days in the hospital 200+ miles away from home, we understand the financial burden placed on families with critically ill children. We want to help families focus on what is most important, their sick child, and not where their next meal is coming from or how they will afford to travel back and forth to their home.

The mission of Ansley's Rainbows of Hope is to ease the financial burden experienced by families of critically ill children receiving care at a distant hospital.

Although we know we cannot take away the pain of seeing their child suffer, we can help meet some of their basic needs. We provide much needed assistance with food, lodging, gas, and other travel expenses for those who qualify for services.

Our Vision

There is no greater gift than hope. It was what kept Robert and I going as we watched our children suffer. These families are hurting, and to be able to love on them, pray with them, and share our hope, means the world.

The **vision** of Ansley's Rainbows of Hope is to offer Christian love and hope to the families of these critical children.

Our community needs love and needs hope. Our prayer is that the families we serve will one day pay it forward. There are endless possibilities if they do!

We strive to meet with each and every family we serve. If it is not possible, due to location, we will try to send someone in our stead. We do not force our faith on anyone, but we do offer to pray with them.

We begin and end every board meeting with prayer. We want to do the Lord's work and we want His guidance in every decision we make. We want our endeavors to support our mission and vision.

Thank you for considering donating to help Rainbow Families. More than anything, we thank you for praying for the families who are facing unfathomable crises with their children.

Nancy Gearhart, the founder and director of Ansley's Rainbow's of Hope.

About the Author

Nancy Gearhart

Nancy Mobley Gearhart was born in Savannah, Georgia. At age 18, she married Robert Gearhart from Volin, South Dakota. They married in Savannah and remained there to build their life together.

Nancy graduated nursing school in 1999 and started her career as a Registered Nurse in the labor and delivery department. She transitioned to working in home healthcare after Ansley passed. In 2012, Nancy graduated with her Masters in Nursing Administration. She currently works in the quality department of a managed care organization.

Nancy started Ansley's Rainbows of Hope in 2014. She continues to serve as the director of the non-profit where she is able to live out her life's calling and passion—offering support and the hope of Christ to families who have lost a child or who have a critically ill or injured child.

Nancy and Robert currently live in Guyton, Georgia. Nancy loves crafting and reading. She and Robert are SCUBA certified, they love to hike—especially to see waterfalls—they love being in the water on jet skis, and traveling and exploring the country.

Nancy would love to hear from you. You can reach her via email at nancy@ansleysrainbows.org.

www.ingramcontent.com/pod-product-compliance
Lightning Source LLC
Chambersburg PA
CBHW070137080526
44586CB00015B/1727